ALL THE TREES WERE BREAD AND CHEESE

THE MAKING OF A REBEL

The autobiography of Harold Horne

Owen Hardisty

First published 1998 by Owen Hardisty
51 Ravenbank Road Luton Bedforshire LU2 8EJ   01582 738268

ISBN 0-9534155-0-3

Printed in Britain by Upstream London SE15 4SE

CONTENTS

Dedication

Dedicated to the memory of Billie Horne, wife of the author, and their youngest daughter Jill Jenkins 1942-1994. Two finer fighters for socialism would be hard to find. Their committment was always tempered with humanity and a sense of humour.

> "The truth that makes man free is
> for the most part the truth that
> men prefer not to hear."

Herbert S Agar

Acknowledgements

To the following for their invaluable advice and support, constructive criticism and technical help.
Ken Cooper, Glyn Morgan, Kim Fisher,
Roger Kitchen – the Living Archive Project at Milton Keynes,
Dr Richard Croucher – Open College Network,
Dr Mark Clapson – Department of Modern History, University of Luton,
Doug Lawrence, Regional Officer AEEU,
Tony Flavell, Brian Duthie, Richard Green – the Trustees of the Harold Horne Memorial Trust, for their help in financing this project.
The Luton News for permission to reproduce photographs.

Edited by Owen Hardisty
Production by Nick Wright

Harold Horne

Harold Horne

PREFACE

Harold Horne's autobiography will be of interest to students of British social and labour history in the twentieth century as well as to the general reader. As an account of the trajectory of a working class activist it takes its place among a small but significant group of other similar accounts given by those whose backgrounds and experiences brought them to join the often embattled ranks of the Communist Party of Great Britain in the years between the wars. It is of interest principally because its subject was a worker from the south of England who was active in the CPGB without holding national office and who therefore felt no great need to indulge in retrospective political self-justification. In this sense, it is clearly important for its honest statement of the views of a 'rank and file' Communist during a period when the CPGB had a significance in British politics and industrial relations (if only because of its links with the USSR) which entirely belied its small membership.

The autobiography is engaging and worthwhile for aspects of its content. The experiences and reading which brought Harold Horne to communism and confirmed him in his views are detailed. Horne's account throws shafts of light on the relatively undocumented life of the National Unemployed Workers' Movement at local level through its amusing account of a branch; the NUWM comes to life in a vivid way. It contains interesting material about the author's family and emotional life, an area neglected in some such autobiographies. There are insights into industrial relations at Vauxhall in the 1940s and 1950s.

Yet perhaps the most striking aspect of the story which follows is its international dimension. Though deeply rooted in the English working class, Harold Horne had an international experience through his time in Spain with the International Brigades, his period in Moscow, and his post-war link with Czechoslovakia. Such experiences remind us that the horizons of Horne's generation of working class Communists were wide, and the importance of what he has to say in his own distinctive and humorous style opens windows onto a wider world.

Richard Croucher Ph.D.

Harold Horne

Introduction

All The Trees Were Bread and Cheese is a unique story of working class life and struggle against adversity and injustice. It's author, Harold Horne, experienced semi-starvation and the brutal and inadequate education system considered suitable for working class children at the time.

As a young man in Willesden during the inter-war years, he suffered the poverty and degradation of unemployment experienced by millions of his generation.

Starting work as a factory hand and later as a page boy at a posh West End club, he was confronted with the startling disparity between the life style of the rich and that of the poor.

Brief tenure of poorly paid and hideously monotonous factory jobs, followed by a return to the dole, became the norm for him. Despair and apathy plagued the ranks of the unemployed, but Harold was one of those who fought back.

His book is a fascinating account of the gradual political awakening of a young worker and the making of a rebel. Told with his own brand of self deprecating humour, he charts his progress from King's Scout to Communism via Speakers' Corner.

His involvement with the Hunger Marchers and the mass demonstrations organised by the National Unemployed Workers Movement brought him six months in Wormwood Scrubs, and the following year he was sent by the Young Communist League to Moscow to study at the Lenin School. Whilst there he met Lenin's widow Krupskaya, and her wise words were to have a lasting influence on his own political thinking

Oswald Mosley's attempt to impose fascism on Britain by the use of his racist blackshirt thugs saw Harold and many other communists leading the heroic resistance which resulted in violent street battles, and culminated in the notorious battle of Cable Street in London's East End.

When General Franco and his fascists attacked Republican Spain, it seemed only natural to Harold that he should continue to resist the spread of fascism and defend democracy. He joined the British battalion of the International Brigade as a volunteer and soldiered on until the end of the Civil War.

In 1940 Harold and his family moved to Luton when he found work at Vauxhall Motors, and where he later became AEU shop stewards convenor at the Bedford Trucks plant at Dunstable.

His tireless work to organise the workforce and his clashes with CJ Bartlett (later Sir Charles) are legendary in the plant. Peter Vigor, former editor of the Vauxhall works magazine recalls that he was puzzled why Harold was not sacked, and adds; "Perhaps it was because he used jokingly to threaten members of the board that, come the revolution, there was a lamp post waiting for them to be hung from."

Harold had a great sense of humour, not in my view, a strong point in Marxists, and when being photographed for the works magazine, insisted on standing against a bleak brick wall as though facing a firing squad.

During the 1950's he re-discovered a love for nature which he had learned as a boy on the banks of the river Brent, and together we fished Tring, Bedford, and a dozen other waters where for a few hours we could forget the turmoil and stress of life in a car factory.

After the death of his wife Billie, and in spite of his superficial cheerfulness, I sensed an underlying melancholy which even fishing trips could not dispel, and in the weeks before his death in 1978 as he strove to finish his book he frequently sought the company of Maureen and myself.

In a tribute by Cambridge historian Lionel Munby and his family which appeared in the *Morning Star* he is remembered as: "one of the finest human beings we have ever known", and they quote Swift's epitaph in Dublin Cathedral.

> "Swift has sailed into his rest;
> Savage indignation there
> Cannot lacerate his breast.
> Imitate him if you dare,
> World-besotted traveller:
> He served human liberty".

Owen Hardisty November 1996

Harold Horne

FORWORD

That I should write a book about my life was first suggested to me by our good friends Alice and Mutyo Teich, whose hospitality my wife and I had twice enjoyed in Prague on holidays.

To these I express my gratitude for implanting the idea, convincing me that it was worthwhile, and giving me the confidence to make the attempt.

After several stabs at it over two or three years, encouraged by my wife Billie and my family, I had come to realise that the book I had envisaged, a political analysis of my life and times, was beyond my capabilities; not least because I had no access to relevant archives, and in any case lacked the energy and drive that would be needed for the painstaking research.

So when our good and close friends Owen and Maureen Hardisty, whom we have known from the early forties, suggested an anecdotal life story, putting on paper some of the stories I had told during 'bull sessions' and 'tell it how it was', trying to recapture the atmosphere of the times for today's generation who know little (and perhaps care less, I sometimes think) I began again, in fits and starts, sometimes going for months without a word written. *All The Trees* is the result.

My greatest thanks then to the above mentioned and many others who kept me going with encouragement and nagging, like Pat who said I owed it to the family if only they ever read it.

If ever it does see the printing press the critics will be quick to point out inaccuracies, especially in dates ,for chronological disorder is one of the stories' most marked features.

It is still the story of my life, and everything told here is the unvarnished truth 'off the top of my head' as I recall it.

I hope the reader will get the message (if there is one) or at any rate be entertained.

Harold Horne 1978

Harold Horne

ALL THE TREES WERE BREAD AND CHEESE

"THE WAR is ending on Monday" said the baker's boy whom I occasionally helped with his round. This was 8 November 1918 and in a few weeks I would be eight years old. Customers would occasionally tip me with a newly washed and polished jam jar which could be exchanged at the grocers for one penny.

For me the war had been remote, some vague affair to which my father and brother George had gone, though I knew that the 'thunder' on moonlight nights and the train loads of wounded men hourly passing over Taylor's Lane bridge in Willesden were part of it. We scrambled for the pennies thrown by the soldiers and sang 'It's a long way to Tipperary' whilst we waited for the next train.

On air raid nights, my younger brother Ted and I would creep from the 'safe' place where we'd been put, which was the corner by the gas stove. Wriggling our way to the window we could get glimpses of planes, bursting shells and occasionally a silver cigar (a German Zeppelin) caught in the searchlights.

Searching for souvenir shrapnel one morning after the night's raid we cheered a squadron of planes roaring out from behind low clouds. We learned later that they had been 'Jerries' when the papers reported that they had dropped their deadly load on a Poplar school killing many children.

Air raid precautions were minimal in working class areas. A bicycled policeman toured the streets blowing his whistle and shouting 'Take cover' which meant get indoors. 'All clear' was sounded by Boy Scouts with bugles

The smashing and looting of a baker's shop owned by a 'nice old couple' who happened to be German was also part of the war.

My eldest sister Emily became a 'Canary Girl' (described by Edith Hall in her *Canary Girls and Stockpots* published by WEA Luton.) Her skin had assumed the bright yellow colouration of the munitions worker through contact with cordite, the explosive charge in shells.

So on 11 November as 11 o'clock approached, our street waited behind it's Union Jack bedecked windows for the gunfire that was to signal the official ending of hostilities. As the first salvo roared out my mother fainted. Coming round she said "I thought the buggers had started again". She must be where I got my tendency to pessimism from.

I was eleven when Dad died, and when Mum became gravely ill I, with my brother Ted, eighteen months my junior, were placed temporarily into a Council Home. The baby, Win, went to a nursery.

The Home was a group of bungalows adjoining an area known as Lower Place, on the banks of the Grand Junction Canal off Acton Lane, a tough district where the children went barefoot and the sort of place you avoided on dark nights.

Immediately on admission, after being briefly consoled by Matron, we were plunged into a hot bath so heavily laced with carbolic – the all purpose disinfectant – that it burned our skin off, de-nitted (the ultimate indignity) and dressed in navy blue jerseys, knickerbockers belted below the knees and stout boots. On Sundays we wore Norfolk jackets with a celluloid Eton collar and a cravat held by a press stud. The boots were useful when attacked by the barefoot boys on our Sunday walk along the canal, their strategic aim being the capture of our straw boaters for skimming across the water.

We tried to escape from the home once and got a good caning for our pains.

Later we were taken from the Home and sent on 'holiday', Ted to an uncle in Rugby and I to relations in Tottenham where I at once resolved to marry my cousin on account of her white silk blouse and beautifully marcel-waved hair. Tottenham to me is still cousin Grace, the Saturday roar from White Hart Lane, ratting on the banks of the river Lea and being forced to kiss the face of a newly dead uncle.

Mum's family

My mother bore ten children – three of whom died in infancy, a not uncommon occurrence in the 1920's. She brought us up as 'respectable' working class.

At an early age we learned that cleanliness is next to Godliness. Children should be seen and not heard (especially when Dad was home) and 'keep your elbows off the table' occasionally enforced with a swish of the cane.

Cleanliness was hard work in the never-ending battle with vermin. The nastiest of these was the bed bug, and how to get rid of 'em a subject of conversation like the weather. They crawled everywhere, up and down and under the wallpaper and in any crack or cranny in wood or plasterwork. They also learned to outflank the paraffin filled tins, in which stood the bed legs when we were having a purge by crawling across the ceiling to drop onto the bed.

When the infestation reached the boundaries of human tolerance, a room would be closed, window cracks and doors sealed with newspaper and sulphur candles lit and left for a whole day. The stink was horrible but we did get the odd unbitten nights sleep.

We lived next to a carter's stable (automobiles were few in number at that time) so sometimes we'd get a big rat in our cage trap in the back yard. This would be taken out into the street to provide diversion for the street's dogs assembled for the purpose.

Every Saturday the house got a scrub and polish. Housework being only for women and kids, Dad, George and Fred went their various ways and battle commenced. While Mum scrubbed floors and tables with scalding water and carbolic soap and Jess polished fireplace and gas stove with 'Zebra' polish eked out with a little vinegar, Ted and I cleaned the cutlery with a brick dust called 'Monkey Brand' which had first to be ground to a powder and then dampened on to a lino-faced emery board. The front door step was whitened with a chalky white hearth stone and God help the one who stepped on it for at least the rest of that day, except Dad of course whose privilege it was. His footprints were unobtrusively obliterated with a further application of hearth stone.

Windows were cleaned with a little paraffin mixed with vinegar. All work finished and inspected, Mother would lie on her bed, her head bound with a warmed strip of brown paper soaked in vinegar – to ease the headache from which she suffered more or less permanently – while we others ate our fish and chips.

Mother worked in a steam laundry all week, coming home Monday evenings to do our washing with the aid of a wood and coal fired copper and a scrubbing board.

She died at the age of 57 from a multiplicity of illnesses which added up to one root cause – overwork. I was to shed my few tears in a Teruel dugout when I read of her death in a week old copy of the *Daily Worker*.

So lived, and died, many women of the working class in the twenties and thirties of this century. Today's women's libbers don't know they are alive. This is not to gainsay the continuing need to combat male chauvinism which remains a blot on our society and an obstacle to human (especially working class) progress.

Quite recently I was looking through a copy of some Women's Lib magazine and came across an article headed, I think, 'How to live without men'. This described in detail (with illustrations) how orgasm could be achieved by the use of various manipulative exercises or mechanical aids.

I'm no prude by any means, quite the contrary, (in fact some of my friends know me as a 'randy old sod') but I am always angered by the trivialisation of great causes and my mind went back then to my boyhood when the fighters for female liberation were, of course the suffragettes and the story of how they fought and won votes for women is well known now.

In the next street to ours lived two middle-aged ladies who were known to be supporters of the suffragette movement and occasionally our gang would, usually on dark nights, divert ourselves by banging on the old dears' front windows yelling interminably "Ole Suffryjet, Ole Suffryjet". One night the door opened suddenly and I found myself dragged into the house where I was sat down on the settee and handed a steaming cup of cocoa. Petrified with fear since it was known to all readers of the gutter press that suffragettes ate small boys, engaged in free love and had a hot line to the German high command; I was shown pictures of women's demonstrations accompanied by a gentle lecture they no doubt considered comprehensible to a twelve year old. Sent on my way with a light kiss (which I supposed was the free love bit), although I had understood little of what they'd talked about, I never again joined the 'anti-suffryjets'.

Perhaps Freud could have explained why I should connect this incident with another which happened soon after and gave me years of nightmares.

On the way to one of our scrumping forays in a country lane at Neasden which is now part of London's North Circular Road, we

happened upon a young woman in some kind of fit (though we
didn't know this at the time). Astride her, a man was squirting
water from his mouth into her face. Now and again he would stop
squirting to slap her hard across the cheek whilst she screamed
obscenities to the delighted crowd. At twelve years old we had
learned something of the sweet mysteries of life, and our heads
were going like a Wimbledon audience between the crazed features
and the exposed genitalia.

At last a policeman arrived and, instead of arresting the
'assailants', as we thought, thanked him and together they
strapped the unhappy girl onto a cart usually reserved for drunks
and corpses and off they went. Sixty years later I still wonder about
it. Perhaps the suffragette's lecture had gone deeper than I knew,
and followed closely by the second incident were, in part
responsible for a tendency for some years – to my later and lasting
regret – to avoid close encounters of the basic kind.

However that may be, the suffragette had taught me, I was to
discover in later years, that equality is for all without regard to sex,
colour or creed. Thank you unknown lady.

But to return to the family. The Hungry Twenties as they are now
known was something more than a phrase to us. We supplemented
our diet of bread and lard or margarine or bread and jam (seldom
both together) with a 'pennorth of specs' part rotten fruit from the
greengrocer, or a halfpenny carrot to gnaw. A part eaten apple or
orange 'fresh' from the gutter was a prize which would bring cries
of "Gis the core" from your mates.

Before you cry 'disgusting little sods', please remember that fruit
was only bought for festive occasions like Christmas, and the great
prize peeping from the toe of the Christmas stocking was an apple
or an orange, together with a packet of revoltingly flavoured
chocolate cigars.

The fat extracted from cocoa in the refining process was sold as
'cocoa butter' and this we ate spread on our bread sometimes.

Occasionally army lorries would unload barrels of herring and
mackerel packed in ice into our school playground, and these were
sold at one farthing per fish (about a quarter of half p in decimal
money).

We stood in long queues for the fish, taking our own wrapping paper. A common trick, especially in midwinter was to gaze appealingly at the soldier guarding the precious cargo and looking even hungrier than you actually were and, if your act was good enough, you might get a few broken pieces thrown in as a free bonus. When this happened, mum would always say "It's the poor as 'elps the poor".

'Unfit for babies' said the label on the condensed milk which used in our tea or cocoa to save on the more expensive 'fresh milk' delivered in zinc plated iron cans or ladled into our own jug from a churn carried on a three-wheeled hand-propelled cart.

The warning on the condensed milk can was widely ignored by the very poor and many an infant's bottle contained this, diluted with warm water. Wailing babies were often quietened with a wad of bread moistened with condensed milk, the resultant mash being tied into a piece of cloth and stuffed into the infant mouth.

In one school I attended hung a streamer which read; "REGULAR DIET MAKES BABY QUIET".

Daily dinners eaten at midday were monotonously predictable, Sunday's joint bought late on Saturday night when prices dropped sharply because few butchers had refrigerators and would sometimes throw in a free breast of mutton or an end piece of flank, mostly fat and bone; this could be rendered down into dripping to fill up a few hungry stomachs at tea times.

With care, the thrifty could make the joint last until Wednesday, becoming cold meat with 'bubble and squeak', mince, and ending with a pennorth of bones added as a succulent stew. A pennorth of stale cakes would sometimes add colour, if little food value to the table at tea time.

As we were not really among the very poor, and as the family grew up and more money came into the house, delicacies like pink salmon, fish paste and cheese appeared more often on the menu.

We children were also regularly dosed with the grey, fish smelling 'Scott's Emulsion', and to effect the proper working of our bowels, huge spoonfuls of Black Treacle mixed with liquorice powder and ground sulphur were forced into protesting stomachs. This ensured us years of chronic constipation.

Dad's Saturday tea was usually a couple of kippers or a smoked haddock. We waited breathless to see who'd get the 'nine inch piers' (ears) or get to soak their specially saved piece of bread in the gravy.

I heard the tale of how Jess, a child at the time, got two whole kippers – in the face when Dad arrived unexpectedly as she bathed in the tin bath before the fire. He followed this up with a clean sweep of the tasselled overmantle, all the ornaments flying out of the window. Kindly neighbours helped to retrieve the pieces. Next week it would be our turn perhaps to similarly help someone.

The biggest growth industry of the time were the pawn shops. Pathetic bundles of clothing, of bed linen, or the old man's suit were pledged for a few coppers on which interest had to be paid when redeemed. Woe betide the woman who couldn't find the cash to redeem father's suit by Friday night at the latest.

When the pawning of war medals had become widespread and a national scandal, the government decreed this illegal though this was widely evaded by pawning a suit or waistcoat which just happened to have a couple of medals attached.

Talk of war medals evokes a memory of an incident which in fact must have preceded that described in the opening sentence of this book perhaps by a few months. One morning my mother announced that she had "seen" a soldier standing and at the foot of her bed before falling to the floor. A day or so later she received the usual War Office telegram saying that George, my eldest brother, had been wounded in France and as I write, the hullabaloo surrounding mum's visit to a French hospital comes back with great clarity.

I have only considered including this story in the book in the light of two other instances of the paranormal(?) I have experienced which I may as well record at this point.

The second set of 'incidents' occurred after Billie and I had lived at Luton for some years and acquired a car. We would sometimes decide at a moment's notice to make the journey to Willesden to visit Billie's mother and sister who then lived at Neasden Lane. Always there were four cups laid out on the table and the kettle boiling. Ma-in-law always knew we were on our way. Indeed on one occasion she had left a note on the front door to say she had just slipped out to buy some cakes for our tea.

The third happened in 1967. One night awakened by a storm, Billie described a dream she had concerning a car accident. She told in detail what had happened, how the car had rolled over and ended right side up in water and described the colour and other details of the car.

In the morning we were to learn that our youngest son Ted had been involved in such an accident and so far as we could estimate, it had occurred at the very time Billie had 'seen' it in her dream. I do not believe in the supernatural and have no particular views on the three incidents described; but they did happen and I would, if required, swear on oath that I have added nothing to make the stories fit the subsequently known facts.

George, whom mum had 'seen' being wounded lay in bed the day long, smoking cigarettes to the detriment of his remaining lung and died, as did many, after exposure to London's notorious 'pea-souper' fogs.

Ted, eighteen months my junior became a fine craftsman in wood work. One of his best works being an illustrated *History of Association Football*. I never saw this work but often heard it talked of. Perhaps it was destroyed when the house in which he lodged was bombed. I will never know now. Ted died on a Rifle Brigade beachhead on the Italian coast in World War II. Of Fred, the politician of the family, I shall speak later.

Cries of Old Willesden

A few of the unemployed, who perhaps had not yet reached the depths of hopelessness and despair, tried their hand at going into business,

The wireless had not yet reached the masses, so there was the song sheet seller who roamed the streets crying his wares;

"ALL THE LATEST SONGS TUPPENCE EACH. ALL A PENNY THE COMICS"

The Muffin Man who rang a hand bell, wooden tray on head and called:

"MUFFINS, CRUMPETS, TWO A PENNY"

The lavender seller who sang a little song, hand held to the side of his mouth;

"WILL YER BUY MY LAVENDER?
SIXTEEN BRANCHES FOR ONE PENNY.

YER BUYS IT ONCE, YER BUYS IT TWICE
IT MAKES YER CLOTHES SMELL VERY NICE"
Or, the Okey Pokey man who sold lumps of ice, rich in colouring
and poor in flavour;
" OKEY POKEY PENNY A LUMP"
The winkle and shrimp man would yell;
"WINKLIES ALL F–R–E–S–H B–O–I–L–E–D adding, in an
obvious reference to the competition, AND THEY AIN'T BEEN
UNDER THE BED ALL NIGHT" .

And, of course, the buskers, often with barrel organ and a
monkey. One old cornet player who only knew 'Abide with Me' and
'The Miners Dream of Home' would be met with coins flung from
windows amid cries of "Ere's a penny, go round the next street."

Some, mind you, were considered good entertainment, like the
performing street party in drag who were reputed to have retired in
comfortable affluence.

We did some busking ourselves with a barrel organ, collecting for
the Lancashire cotton workers who were on strike in 1931 against
wage cuts. Once outside a pub we sang songs accompanied by a
portable organ. Billie, in a bit of overacting, leaned on the
instrument which slowly collapsed with sounds like a steam-
rollered cat. Laughter, cries of 'encore', were followed by the biggest
collection ever. But despite all our entreaties Billie could never be
persuaded to repeat this fine performance.

Health and wealth

If more people die today with coronary heart disease, destroyed
liver and kidneys and other ailments, undoubtedly due in part to
over-consumption of mass produced foods from which most of the
health giving properties have been extracted (to be sold as bye-
products supposedly to correct ailments brought about by the
extraction of certain elements in the first place). In my young days
it was the other way round, people lacked the calories and vitamins
because they did not get enough to eat.

One result was tuberculosis, known then as consumption, to have
which was equivalent to a death warrant.

CARNET DE HONOR

SE le nombra Combatiente de Honor de la 35 División del Ejército Popular Regular, como Voluntario de la Libertad. Por sus acciones fué en nuestra nación expresión firme de la avanzada del Frente Popular y de la Democracia del Mundo, en lucha contra el fascismo invasor.

Los soldados de la División, todos los españoles, no olvidarán jamás los que con ellos defendieron la independencia del suelo nacional, cubriéndose de gloria en las batallas en que intervinieron.

Al lanzar nuestro ¡Vivan los Voluntarios Internacionales! afirmamos que la República Española conseguirá su independencia total.

España, octubre de 1938.

El Jefe de la División   El Comisario Delegado de G

COMBATIENTE Harold Horne Sargento

FILIACION

Estatura
Pelo
Ojos
Cara
Barba
Nariz
SEÑAS PARTICULARES

(Firma del interesado)
Fecha de nacimiento 31-12-1910
Lugar de nacimiento Willesden London
Nacionalidad Ingles
Profesión Chofer Coach fitter
Estado civil Casado (1 hija)
DOMICILIO: País Inglaterra
Pueblo Willesden London
Calle Church Rd   núm. 89
Partido Político Antifascista
Fecha de entrada en las B. I. 9-8-1937
Fecha de entrega de la libreta 25-8-1937

— 2 —

▲ **Presented at the final parade of the International Brigade Barcelona 1938**

Right Harold Horne's brigade pay book

Harry Pollit, general secretary of the Communist Party meets Harold Horne, Luton Town Hall 1949. Photo *Luton News*

Arrival at a house of the glass enclosed hearse drawn by two black horses meant that some poor soul had succumbed to one or other of these 'Acts of God'.

Diseases like whooping cough, measles, scarlet fever and diptheria now held at bay by antibiotics and other drugs, were common killers. I recall discussing with a doctor early in 1948 the coming of the new National Health Service. A defender of free enterprise he declared his opposition to becoming, as he put it, a 'civil servant'. He left behind him a thriving multi-doctored practice. It seems that people hate change until it is forced upon them by circumstance.

In the Good Old Days it cost at least a shilling (5p) to visit the doctor and half a crown (12p) if you called him out. In some areas there would be a doctor who charged half price. These were known as 'Tanner Doctors'.

Illness, particularly of the breadwinner was perhaps the most feared prospect facing working people, so they tended to succumb to the advertised claims of various (mostly useless) patent nostrums.

At a time when women's place,when not at the scrubbing board, was in bed, the resulting pregnancies were attacked by a bewildering variety of remedies. Slippery Elm bark, bought in long strips at the chemists and followed by a stiff gin and a hot bath were part of the folk lore of the time. Even an accidental 'fall down the stairs' was not unknown to the more desperate, and if all else failed there were women whose names, like bookies' runners, were spoken in whispers, who would do the job for a fee. This usually involved a crochet hook or knitting needle with a consequent high mortality rate from peritonitis .

Sheaths were suspect for it was widely believed that the manufacturers had by law to provide a pin hole in a certain percentage of their products. Titled ladies wrote articles in the papers commending the new butter substitute called margarine and telling how a nourishing stew could be made with a pennyworth of bones and an onion (as if we didn't know). Thousands of kiddies displayed the knock knees and bandy gait that indicates rickets. Rickets is caused by starvation.

No wonder that when I got to politics I sang the *Rebel Song* with feeling. This song goes in part:

Harold Horne

". . . song of love and hate
of love unto the lowly
and hatred to the great".

School days

I disliked school: a feeling no doubt heartily reciprocated by the staff, mostly frustrated sadists who believed firmly in the adage 'Spare the rod, Spoil the child'.

Two subjects most detested were arithmetic and games, as sport was called at our school. I'll give my vote to any party which pledges to shift all sport exclusively to a fourth channel.

Arithmetic is another story. Elementary education in my day was primitive and the organisational structure worse. Housed in great Victorian three-storied buildings, infants five to about eight or nine were on the ground floor, big girls on the middle floor, and big boys on the top.

As I had for some long period to attend a local clinic due to an eye malfunction euphemistically known as 'blight', I missed most of the numbers' lessons which always followed scripture in the morning. Consequently on reaching big boys' class one I never knew whether I was on foot or horseback. The teacher of this class was a right bitch and I of course, just what the doctor ordered for the release of her frustrations.

Each morning she'd have me out front counting on a child's bead frame wearing the pointed 'dunces cap' whilst she repeatedly lashed the back of my legs with a thin springy cane.

After some weeks of this I decided I'd had enough, so when one morning she called me out, I let her have two inkwells right in the chest; one red and one blue. The ink ran down her white silk blouse till she looked like a titless Britannia without the fireman's helmet.

Calling loudly for aid she got me out into the Assembly Hall where a school leavers' exam was in progress. The boys brightened visibly as I cleared a table of assorted scientific instruments in about two minutes flat.

At university I believe they call it being 'sent down'; I got thrown down the stone steps (about a hundred of then I think) and told not to come back. So I got a few weeks holiday until the Director of Education called to utter dire warnings about future conduct. After that, nobody ever tried to teach me arithmetic. I managed tolerably well in most other subjects and got by until the day came when I shook the dust of school from my itching feet. School had taught me one thing though; to hate and fight against injustice, a lesson I've tried never to forget.

Summer holidays

Summer holidays were, next to Christmas, the year's high spot, seen in retrospect to have occurred in hot sunny weather. No radio or TV cameras or music centres we made our own magic and were seldom bored in the way that today's generation seem to be.

I recall a week at Southend with mum and the odd Sunday school outing to Bricket Wood. Apart from these I never really had a proper holiday until long after I married. If you were lucky enough to be born in the East End of London you could get a working holiday in the Kentish hop fields.

A few more than usually deprived could get the odd holiday through various charities. A huge poster which dominated the hoardings at one time appealing for funds, pictured ragged urchins holding up handfuls of grass for their parents' inspection, "look mummy, grass!"

We spent a large part of the summer at 'The Spinney', a natural widening of the river Brent quite close to where the North Circular Road now runs at Neasden. The hawthorn and dog rose abounded and we were fond of chewing the new spring leaves of the hawthorn which we called for some reason "bread and cheese". Whilst chewing we chanted with Lewis Carrol:

"If all the land was paper
And all the sea was ink
And all the trees were bread and cheese,
What would we have to drink?"

In this landscape dominated by a burning rubbish tip and a disused chalk quarry, generations of kids had created their own adventure playground where we became Sexton Blake, Tom Mix or

Buffalo Bill and, naturally, experimented with sex.

Better even than sex, would you believe was to paddle down the river on planks, the Brent having become magically transformed into some African river, ending up in the quarry caves carved from the chalk where we cooked delicious meals of roast potatoes lifted en passant from a greengrocer's display, followed by steaming mugs of tea or cocoa made from river water which today would drop you in your tracks. Barring the odd dead cat, England's rivers were then relatively unpolluted and full of fish which we sometimes caught and ate.

The Welsh Harp, the big reservoir edging the A5 near Hendon was another unofficial lido, where on hot summer nights midnight bathing was the done thing. Later in the 1930s you could look across the water to a large green space with grass like a billiard table. It had swings and roundabouts, a refreshment kiosk and no people, and was said to have cost £60,000, "wasting our money" moaned the ratepayers disporting themselves on our side.

Evenings we played the usual street games. A great favourite was 'Knocking down Ginger'. We selected as victims the most child-hating adults in the street, knocking at their door we'd run and hide and then, giving them time to get sit down, we'd knock again and again.

A refinement of this game was to tie a string to the knocker operated by a boy from the branches of a nearby tree. This however fell into disfavour when unexpected side effect in the shape of a burly copper calling "Come down you little sod", administering a smart cuff round the ear and hauling you off to your Dad who waited belt at the ready.

Girls played hopscotch, ring-a-ring-o-roses and skipping, and God help any boy mad enough to join in.

In only one game were girls allowed. Called 'Relesso' it was usually played after dark and consisted of two teams, one of which hid and to be found piecemeal by the other. We did a lot of our practical work on the sex education front in this game, and comparing notes afterwards the braggarts who'd nearly but not quite made it would be made to repeat their experience in vivid detail. Increasing in eroticism with each telling, the liars often finished up with a parental belting .

Harold Horne

The Penny Pictures

Saturday was Bug Hutch day. Grasping our penny admission fee we joined the queue at the cinema in High Road, Willesden.

Handing over our penny we got a bag of chalk-like Edinburgh rock or a stick of liquorice and surged forward in search of seats as far as possible from the evil smelling lavatories. First the cartoons, Pip Squeak and Wilfred, the popular heroes of a comic strip in the *Daily Mirror*, I think, or Felix the cat followed by a comedy starring Charlie Chaplin, Harold Lloyd or Buster Keaton.

Then the Big Picture. This usually starred Tom Mix, Eddie Polo or Douglas Fairbanks playing opposite Mary Pickford, the World's Sweetheart, Lillian Gish or Dolores Del Rio. The Big Picture was always a serial and went on interminably.

It took Lillian Gish about three weeks to reach the killer rapids as, silent (talking films were not yet) and beautifully coiffured, she lay on the ice floe – whilst the hero racked his brains and bust a gut – till came the great Saturday when his efforts were crowned with success.

Film heroes were always clean living American cowboys. The baddies you knew by their straw sombreros and pidgin English spoken with a Spanish accent.

"Tell her no move, tarantula no bite" choked the greaser as All American thumbs bit into his windpipe. Tom Mix could have taken the place apart with his bare hands in the time it took that spider to reach Mary Pickford's plunging neckline from the conveniently placed bunch of bananas. Brinkmanship was the name of the game, So Tom knelt on one knee six gun in hand aimed at Mary's left tit. TO BE CONTINUED NEXT WEEK.

Yelling our disappointment we went home to dinner speculating whether the tarantula would end up spattered on the wallpaper or Mary be minus a nipple.

Being Prepared

At twelve or thereabouts, I joined a scout troop attached to a local church. Main activities were Church Parades and athletics. The number of proficiency badges on your sleeve were in direct ratio to energy consumed in athletics. Run by muscular youths whose aim seemed to be to inculcate the spirit of *mens sana in copore sano*, I soon got fed up with this, (the athletics I mean) and transferred a troop attached to a local golf club. Known as Caddy Scouts you were supposed to caddy for the club members, though few ever did, and I still don't know a mashie from an old umbrella.

With film shows –where we took turns to operate the projector – free camping and outings, I soon got covered in proficiency badges. Maybe due more to my looks (I was a comely lad then) than skill at the tests I became a King's Scout. One of the requirements of a King's Scout was to hand over your bicycle 'In the name of the King' to any policeman or serving officer. Though I'd cycle slowly past all policemen flashing my gold lanyard, fame and glory always evaded me.

I was still in this scout troop when, at the age of fourteen I became a messenger boy at the Great Wembley Empire Exhibition of 1924 /1925. The messenger boys had to wear scout uniform at all times. I quickly learned how to get free cigarettes and chocolate from the hundreds of vending machines which in those days were less 'fiddle proof' than now. I collected a regular supply of chocolate, cocoa, Shredded Wheat and various other free samples of products from Britain's Colonies and Dominions.

In the Palace of Industry, of all places, there was a stand called 'The Alliance of Honour' manned by men with leery eyes who handed out leaflets to young male passers by. This leaflet which in heavy type proclaimed that "IGNORANCE IS NOT INNOCENCE", invited one to sign the pledge at the bottom of the form to eschew the delights of masturbation. As I knew not the meaning of this word I remained ignorant though not, of course, innocent.

I think I am right in saying that the first FA Cup match played at Wembley was between Charlton and West Ham. Two of us had got ourselves ensconced in one of the Stadium's great domes overlooking the pitch. After about twenty minutes boredom conquered us and we turned to the other side and watched the antics of a policeman on a white horse making frequent sallies with his long sword stick into a vast crowd of disappointed fans who had failed to make the turnstiles. The horse became a national hero overnight and got nearly as much press coverage as the match itself.

The Exhibition was run like the Empire it purported to portray, by ex-service brasshats who spent their time between lunch and golf sending minutes and memos to each other in triplicate.) After two years it closed, having made a loss of many millions of pounds, a portent perhaps of the imminent liquidation of the British Empire itself. A few years later I was to take a somewhat less benign view of the Empire and of mounted policemen with sword sticks.

In long trousers now

Just before leaving school I was called into the assembly hall to be interviewed by three old men and a woman who glared fixedly at me and one of whom barked "Well my boy, you leave school next week. What do you want to be?"

Not having been warned in advance about this career guidance bit I was petrified, not knowing what I should answer. I said "Engineer, sir" thinking this had to do with driving steam locomotives. So when he asked "What kind of engineer" I could have died. When he began to run through a list of kinds of engineer I seized on one which sounded familiar and said "Electrical engineer".

Relief all round. That was another career sorted out, and I was handed a ready-typed letter to the manager of the Bowden Wire Company in Acton, given a short lecture by the lady member on the subjects of piety, sobriety, diligence and "Don't be late in the mornings".

I lasted just one week at Bowden Wire. Wages were ten shillings (50p) per week of fifty hours and the work boring and repetitive, (the new Bedeaux System now called Time and Motion Study was just being introduced in Britain) so I packed it in – swearing never again to do factory work.

No dole then for teenagers or for that matter adults if you packed up your job, so I kicked around for a week or so until the scoutmaster found me the job at the Wembley Exhibition described in the previous chapter.

Harold Horne

After Wembley folded, I became a page boy at a top people's club in Mayfair known as the Garden Club. Situated in Curzon Street opposite No. 10 where lived the Duke and Duchess of York – who later were to become King George VI and the present Queen Mother – the club servants would crowd the windows to watch the royal comings and goings, always preceded by the rolling down of a red carpet.

If you watched *Upstairs, Downstairs* on TV you'll have some idea of the atmosphere of the times.

I slept on a ricketty bed in a room no larger than a fair-sized cupboard and received nocturnal visits from some of the stillroom maids. But I was so dumb – and always looking gift horses in the mouth – that we never ever got down to 'brass tacks' as they say. In fact I remained virtually a virgin until about the age of twenty four. I reckon the saying 'If youth would and age could' was specially coined for me.

I spent my off duty time in the cheaper West End cafes and amusement arcades in the Edgware Road, usually ending with a meal of pie and eels at a cheap restaurant next door to the Metropolitan Music Hall, sometimes it would be the old Victoria Palace where for 5p you could get a seat in the gods, five perfumed and evil-smelling cigarettes and a bag of sweets.

That was really living it up. You could see all the great stars there; Marie Lloyd, Yesta Tilley, Gertie Gitana, Harry Tate (whose Heath Robinson type mousetraps filled the whole stage and brought the house down), Max Miller and many others.

One night, feeling I suppose a bit above myself I arrived at the club in a hansom cab which stopped at the front door, and got a telling off from the manager for "trying to ape your betters".

Then there was the case of the red kipper. Staff meals were served in the kitchen according to a strict protocol based on a hierarchical system at the apex of which sat, I believe, the Head Butler.

Two Italian waiters, reputedly anarchists, noticing one morning that I had only one kipper, demanded that I be given another like everyone else. A deathly hush, eyes popped, forks stopped in mid air; "Page boys get one" cried the second cook, "It's orders." Getting up from their places the two Italians repeated "Two for the boy or we wreck the joint". Like magic a second kipper appeared and thereafter I always got two.

My first political lesson? Perhaps, though I didn't recognise it then. I'd thought of anarchists as people who threw bombs at kings and things, and never dreamed that kippers for page boys came into their programme.

After the club I worked as errand boy for a series of butchers' shops and grocers. It was from this grocery that I was able to witness the opening rounds of the great General Strike of 1926.

Nine days that shook Britain – and me.

The grocery was perched on the bridge at Neasden Station on the Metropolitan line. On 1 May 1926 the General Strike begun, and I watched from a back window as pickets with huge red flags stopped the trains coming from Stanmore, South Harrow and Northwood, the newly developing Metroland where lived stockbrokers and civil servants in bowler hats and pin stripe trousers.

Just as it began to get interesting I was ordered to take my box tricycle to Marble Arch, a few miles off to pick up some supplies which, of course, had failed to arrive. So off I pedalled along Harrow Road and Edgware Road to the wholesalers near Marble Arch.

Not much sign of the revolution predicted by the papers, just sullen groups of workers occasionally booing the troops and armoured cars laid on for their benefit. The few buses that were running were driven by university undergraduates (few workers got to the universities in 1926) and were accompanied by a policeman on the front seat. In the Harrow Road there was a bus overturned and mounted police were charging into the crowd, batons flailing.

Arriving at my destination I was met by a picket leader who gave me a wedge of currant cake and a short lecture on working class solidarity and sent me homewards empty but happy.

This is experience must have affected me more than I realised at the time for when I was later to study the theory of the State as a weapon of the boss class it made sense.

After all I had seen it in action against the workers.

Harold Horne

Coming to politics

My second eldest brother Fred was the politician of our family. He had joined the Independent Labour Party and became a respected Labour councillor in the Urban District of Willesden. He eventually became an area organiser for the Transport Workers' Union and died a few months before he was due to retire.

We began to read the *Daily Herald* and *Reynolds News* on Sundays. Our kitchen wall was graced by a multi-coloured portrait of Ramsey Macdonald, later replaced by Clement Attlee when MacDonald betrayed his class and formed the so-called National Government in 1931.

Having joined the Communist Party in 1930 I began to read some of Fred's books, especially the historical novels of writers like Upton Sinclair, whose *Jungle* tells the story of the inhuman conditions in Chicago's stockyards and Jack London's *Iron Heel* portraying the rise of fascism. I never read a simpler exposition of the economic principles of socialism than that described in Robert Tressell's *Ragged Trousered Philanthropists!*

When people spoke of one law for the rich and one for the poor I preferred the way Anatole France put it:

"The law in its majestic equality forbids the rich as well as the poor to beg in the streets, sleep under bridges and to steal bread".

I learned a lot about the reality behind the headlines and began to grasp the essence of the Socialist idea from such 'light' reading; though such frivolous study was not highly regarded in party circles of the day I am sure that such works should be more widely promoted as an introduction to left-wing politics.

From an anthology edited by Upton Sinclair and titled *The Cry for Justice* I learned of the battles waged by the common people throughout the world, like the Kentucky miners holed up in snow bound mountains awaiting attack by company thugs, and the cemetery in Detroit where lie the bodies of lads killed by company police for trying to unionise Ford and General Motors. Seeing our own police smashing the skulls of desperate-eyed men in broken shoes stuffed with old newspapers against the cold and wet made me want to join the fight. One result of my unemployed activity being that I got on the employers' Black List and was out of work for three years (more than four I suppose, if you count the odd month here and there).

I suppose we were the Angry Young Men of the thirties. We didn't just write about it we tried to DO something. We marched, and marched, and marched. To the Public Assistance Committee; to County Hall, home of the London County Council and to Parliament. Or as near as the 'Cossacks' as we called the mounted police would let us get.

Once, a score or so of us in retreat from a baton charge, found ourselves in a posh restaurant where dinner was being served. The diners, elegant in their soup and fish, eyed these strange creatures in caps and mufflers fearfully. Huddled against the far wall they, no doubt, thought the revolution had come. One of us made a short speech outlining the claims of the unemployed and pointing out *en passant*, that what each of them had paid for one night's dinner would have kept an unemployed family for weeks. Then the coppers arrived. After a brief argument with the manager they left, handing out only black looks and muttered threats.

That manager was a smart fellow, telling the police that he was quite happy to have us he then served us with coffee and sandwiches. He had, no doubt, done a quick estimate of the cost of repairs to his dining room should a battle take place and had possibly seen himself joining our ranks on the morrow if it did. He even gave us the 'All clear' when all was quiet outside, and we left after thanking him sincerely and promising to remember him 'come the revolution'.

Say Hunger March to today's telly-fed generation and they think at once of Jarrow. The Jarrow March was in fact, possibly the least effective of all the Hunger Marches despite it's newsworthiness. ('The town that died'). In desperation the town where the entire population were unemployed sent it's marchers to London led by the fiery, red headed MP Ellen Wilkinson. You don't preach to starving women and children so all possible support was given to the Jarrow march, though we regretted their decision to go it alone.

In London the marchers got bags of sympathy from Whitehall and great promises. And Jarrow stayed dead until around 1938 to 1939 when ships were again needed to meet the growing threat from Hitler's Germany, (or as some in high places hoped, to help

Hitler crush the Soviet Union and restore 'Order' at home).

The Prince of Wales paid a visit to miners hovels in the Rhondda Valley, providing the press with a ready made headline when he allegedly said "Something MUST BE DONE". Of course nothing WAS done and conditions got worse. Unbelievably, you can still find the odd one or two among my contemporaries who believe that Edward's subsequent decision to abdicate the English throne was forced upon him less because of his decision to wed Mrs Wallis Simpson, than because of those spoken words which 'they' had bitterly resented.

The National Unemployed Workers Movement, however, knew that no saviour from on high was going to deliver us so the unemployed fought on.

Average pay at this time was around £2.50. Dole money was about 75p and to get it you had to prove you were 'genuinely seeking work'. After one year you were subjected to the hated Means Test before being granted Transitional Benefit. Inspectors would visit your home prying into cupboards and even under beds to see if you had anything you could sell. Perhaps you'd have two saucepans; well, you only needed one. I remember gleefully forcing one such to remove his bowler hat on crossing my threshold. A small but satisfying victory

Tin Pan Alley continued to turn out the slush of the *'Every Cloud has a Silver Lining'* variety while from America (where else?) came *'Buddy can you spare a dime'*. This song, much criticised in our circles, nonetheless echoed the growing despair of the unemployed in Britain.

"Once I built a tower up to the sun
Brick and rivet and lime,
Once I built a tower,
Now it's done,
Buddy can you spare a dime?"

But for Britain's unemployed our begging days were over. Marches got bigger and angrier. Our banners bore the slogans "WE REFUSE TO STARVE IN SILENCE" and "WORK OR FULL Maintenance.

In 1932 occurred the biggest Hunger March of all. Coming from all corners of Britain, they assembled in Hyde Park to be welcomed by an estimated quarter of a million people and a massive show of police power. Many of the marchers had carried sticks to help them on the long journey. Before entering the park the police issued an ultimatum to which, after much argument, the March Council acceded and passed instructions down the ranks to that effect

Agents provocateur got busy trying to persuade the marchers to ignore the order and to fight their way into the park. In this they failed signally, such was the discipline of the marchers.

As I write these lines (in September 1978) an article has appeared in the *Guardian* exposing a decision by the Lord Chancellor to withdraw at the request of Scotland Yard, the police report of these events which had been made public under the fifty year rule, despite their having been public for eleven years.

At the time of which I write, the existence of police spies and provocateurs was well known to all left-wing activists and now of course, is widely known. As this menace to political freedom grew the Communist Party published a special pamphlet entitled *The agent provocateur in the Labour Movement*, a copy of which I believe I still have amongst my old books and pamphlets.

Unless I am mistaken, which I think unlikely as the events described were a great sensation at the time, the matters contained in the police report refer to an alleged plot to use the occasion of the presence of the Hunger Marchers in London to initiate large scale rioting, burn down public buildings and commit a series of offences against Law and Order that could, if proven, result only in loss of public support for the unemployed campaign. And, incidentally justify the prosecution of their leaders who would be expected to receive long prison terms in consequence

The 'plot' became public in the following manner.

During a meeting of the March Council, which was held to discuss the next stages of the campaign, a sealed envelope was handed to Wal Hannington which, when he opened it, proved to be a kind of 'Zinoviev letter' outlining in detail the alleged riot plans.

Hannington at once recognised the document to be a forgery and read it out in full to the assembled delegates. A decision was taken and effected there and then to destroy the document. A wise move this proved to be when the next morning police and Special Branch officers raided the Great Ormond Street offices of the NUWM, taking away high piles of papers and correspondence. Failing to find what they were looking for I fancy some heads must have rolled in the Special Branch after that fiasco.

Everyone should view with concern, especially in these days of computerised intelligence, the demands of some high-ranking police officials for greater powers to deal with problems of 'security'. The price of liberty we all know is indeed eternal vigilance.

So the great march on Parliament went ahead with a massively unprecedented show of police strength. Ambulances stood ready down the entire length of Whitehall. Spoiling for a fight, the police horses were charged at the crowd, their riders' batons lashing out indiscriminately at demonstrators and innocent by-standers alike.

I happened to be among a large group that broke through the police lines and got into Parliament Square. As this happened on several occasions during the evening, many of us concluded that we had been deliberately allowed to break the police ranks so that we could be more easily beaten up or arrested. At any rate, I got myself badly beaten up by about a dozen foot police in a dark corner of the Square and recall, just before losing consciousness the flash of a press camera and the immediate smashing of the camera by a mounted policeman's baton.

When I awoke I was forced out of the Square by a mountie who trotted after me the whole length of Birdcage Walk giving me another tap whenever I tried to pause for breath.

I made my way then to the rendezvous meeting in Hyde Park where a huge crowd was hearing the leaders' reports on the days happenings.

Here again, the secret agents were at work and calls were being made for a march on Buckingham Palace but after a rousing speech by Hannington, head swathed in bandages, we marched off back to our localities where the marchers were being fed and slept in school halls.

Willesden had the honour of accommodating the Scottish marchers, a grand bunch whose stirring music on pipe and drum kept up our spirits and straightened our backs when we were near to dropping.

Billie had played a leading part in the hospitality arrangements, securing halls and sleeping accommodation and organising the distribution of food and cigarettes. Almost asleep on her feet she went the rounds with words of encouragement as she always did on all the demo's and Hunger Marches. No one ever heard a word of complaint from her. Mind you – sometimes she would sink into a chair after a hard day's battle and say to me "; think we must be bloody mad" but she would be there next day bright and early, ready for the next round.

Offices and even homes of known left wingers were under constant surveillance. The *Daily Worker* which then was published from an old warehouse in Tabernacle Street in East London, sometimes photographed the Special Branch men through the front window.

We would sell the *Daily Worker* on the streets with the cry; "It must be true, there's a copper sitting in the office all the time".

I had on occasion spotted interference with my mail; some bungler had replaced two letters posted from different areas in the wrong envelopes.

Even now, when I am old and virtually inactive, I have grounds for believing that my telephone conversations are monitored.

Serving a prison sentence (of which more later) I was enabled through a 'screw's' negligence to read my police report. This described me as "Honest and sober and from a respectable family background". Just as I began to wonder what I was doing here came the punch line, "but associates with Communists and other revolutionaries".

The Judge at my Old Bailey trial had constantly interrupted my speech to the jury with remarks like "You are not on trial for your political views there are no political trials in England ".

The Willesden branch of the National Unemployed Workers Movement had managed to acquire the use at a low rent of an old condemned house. Here we conducted the daily business of typing claims and preparing representations before the Court of Referees, collecting the weekly half pence membership fees and selling hot dogs made up with cheap sausages and yesterday's rolls. Here we also planned local campaigns like chaining ourselves to the railings of the local Police Court; finding ourselves inside the court next morning on breach of the peace and obstruction charges.

Harold Horne

Barricading, and day and night guarding of houses where the tenants were to be evicted was also a frequent activity.

I suppose all organisations have their nutters and Walter Mittys and sometimes I thought we had more than our fair share. I include the following without malice; for though the characters mentioned did tend to inhibit logical discussion, they also provided some light relief in our darker moments.

Non-active periods might be taken up by discussing over cups of tea in the rooms, the probable date of the coming Revolution Forecasts ranged from next Friday to five years. Whilst the five-year-pessimists were eyed askance, the next-Friday advocates usually got demolished when it was pointed out that Friday was dole money day, and therefore at least one day's postponement would be necessary.

Always in these discussions spoke up the poor souls fighting their own private revolutions.

The little man in the battered bowler who had his speech word perfect, and repeated it at any time he had an audience of one or more. This speech described the manner in which unscrupulous relatives had robbed him of a violin maker's business, and if the NUWM would help him regain his property he'd be worth, "not undreds, but fahsands".

There was Smith alias Robinson alias Swartz. You never knew which one he was being at any given time. You'd say "Hello Smith" and get a long "Psst" in reply, indicating in a whisper that he was now being Robinson who had managed to infiltrate MI5, or Swartz, an undercover agent of Germany's Red Front fighters. I last met him in Spain being a stretcher bearer in an American field dressing station, and speaking with a strong accent of the Bronx. At least his heart was in the right place.

And the anarchist who claimed – in Hyde Park during the General Strike – to have engaged a tank driver in conversation, whilst he fondled a Mauser pistol in his pocket. "One shot and I could have started the revolution" he apologised; omitting to mention that the Mauser was minus a firing pin and anyway had no ammunition.

Then we got down to business. A speaker, perhaps from headquarters would speak on 'the situation' outlining the campaigns to come and proposing some local actions. Discussion followed and was replied to by the speaker; whilst in the background could be heard the constantly reiterated, "Not 'undreds but farsands".

Life would be dull without it's eccentrics, as I further found out at Vauxhall. But about that, more later.

How I got to be a communist

We now go back a year or two to 1928/9. My friend Harry and I had become clothes conscious affecting blue Melton overcoats – barrel shaped from the waist down, blue serge suits, pointed shoes known as 'winkle pickers', wide bottomed trousers (Oxford bags) with the whole topped off with a natty bowler hat for Sundays.

Weekdays we wore check caps with black peaks called 'Black Bottoms' worn low over the eyes – all bought on the 'never never'.

Looking like a couple of pox doctor's clerks we hit the town. On Sundays we had a regular pub crawl, starting in Willesden and visiting favourite pubs right up to Marble Arch. With beer at 2p a pint, cigarettes five for 11p, a hunk of fresh bread and delicious pub cheese we could, by walking home and bussing some, still have enough for a hot pie and tea when we got back to Willesden: the night out having cost us about 15 pence each.

A few pints under our belts and we'd make for Hyde Park's famous Speakers' Corner to join the hecklers. We wasted little time on the religious fanatics who included a seedy little man holding up a splinter of wood which he claimed came from the Cross of Calvary. We enjoyed ourselves with a paranoiac known only as Charley who weekly made an identical speech. His regular audience had the speech word perfect, and used to chide him when he got behind; or would take over where Charlie left off if a call of nature required his temporary absence.

A bewildering variety of Socialists, Anarchists, Free Thinkers and so-called communists attracted us, as we had recently picked up a copy of the *Daily Worker*, had read the whole of it's four pages and wanted to know more.

One chap who described his nightly battle to keep the rats from his sleeping children and beat them (the rats) to the breakfast table would always end his speech with these words: "You fools, you mugs, rise like lions from your slumber" and quickly vanish into the crowd at the approach of the Law.

But the greatest of all was Jarvis. On his rostrum were the words 'International Socialism'. A spectacular figure, dressed head to toe in black with a wide-brimmed Homburg he wore always, and fluttering beside him on the platform, a gigantic red flag. Jarvis, who had a stentorian voice you could hear nigh to Oxford Circus, was never stumped for an answer. He commanded the biggest audiences and loved every minute of it.

"Talk about the Red Army" he'd cry; "Why, in my bedroom in the Royal Borough of Kensington we get the Red Army every night, up and down the wallpaper in serried ranks".

Once when a young woman of the upper classes protested the presence of the red flag, Jarvis stopped, looked in mock amazement at the flag. "Red flag lady? Red flag? That flag you see is a white flag. What you see is the reflection of your ruby lips".

After the nonsense he gave 'em what they came for. His eloquent description of "The glorious lands to be" when at last the sleeping giant of labour had awakened to cast off the capitalist chains, held vast audiences spellbound.

All great fun, but not getting us to where the real action was at, in the Communist Party. The Party at that time did not hold meetings at Speakers Corner, considering it a bit of a vaudeville show (which it was); so in the end we bought two copies of the *Daily Worker* from a seller at the Park gates and sent off our applications for membership.

Soon we received each a letter from Harry Pollitt giving the address of the North West London Communist Party and inviting us to write a short letter to King Street (party centre) explaining why we had decided to become members of the party.

I hope to God the archivists at King Street don't keep all those letters. I blush with shame even now when I think of mine, all about the "great task of freeing the world from bondage". I bet it gave the apparatchiks a good belly laugh.

North West London's communists rented an empty shop in the slum area of Kilburn. Among the leading members we met at our first meeting there were Emile and Elinor Burns, Idris and Dora Cox and Claude Berridge, who was later to become a national official in the Amalgamated Engineering Union. I recall with gratitude the help and friendship extended to me.

Introduced to the meeting and being declared officially members, we listened to some (for us) incomprehensible discussion about the 'Prague resolution' (unemployment in the capitalist world); the Scottsboro Boys (A legal lynching of some black youths in America's Deep South on framed-up rape charges), and the expulsion of two members of the Party Executive for opposing the party line. Some organisational talk, and we were enjoined to report at the next meeting on the situation at our work place, which happened to be a power station construction job.

The meeting ended with the singing of the *Internationale*.

Next week Harry reported that the workers on our job were "Absolutely opposed to Communism". This was met with roars of laughter, and we felt shamed and hurt until kindlier comrades explained that party work usually operated on a slightly less lofty plane.

At one meeting where the setting up of industrial groups as the basic party unit was discussed the only postman present asked "What about the postal workers?"

"Hardly an industry" said Berridge.

"What is it then, a fucking pastime?"

After the laughter had died down postmen became officially, at least in North West London, industrial workers.

Our first public activity was a demonstration at the annual Air Show held at Hendon Airdrome. Thousands of family parties with picnics were there and we gave out some leaflets which explained the role of the RAF which even then was bombing India's North West frontier and how it was to be used in a war against the Land of Socialism.

As the first planes roared overhead Claude Berridge rose to speak. We didn't want to spoil their enjoyment, he began, but . . . and that was as far as he got. Rising as one man, a great part of the crowd yelling "Bugger off . . . Bloody Bolshies" and began to throw bottles and stones whilst we tried to effect a dignified retreat. As we reached the exit I could feel warm blood on the back of my head.

Billie Horne in the 1930's
Always where the action was

Harold and Billie relaxing with 'Uncle Joe, Billie's mother and son Ted at the Munby's home at West Wickham. 1963

Neighbours and friends 1965
Billie Horne, Maureen Hardisty and Ethel Smith

Harold demonstrating the art of busking. Al Jolson did it this way

With his eldest daughter Pat at her wedding, St Thomas's Church, Stopsley 6 August 1958

The last picture of Harold Horne, with Maureen Hardisty, at Brill steam rally 3 September 1978

Some idiot was talking of "your first baptism of fire, comrade". All I wanted to do was lie down.

The only other case of 'spontaneous' violence I remember was press-inspired, and concerned the incident of the frigate *Amethyst*. which had been up to no good in the Yangtze river and had been fired on by Chinese shore batteries. A crowd of inflamed Vauxhall workers had assembled for our weekly factory gate meeting. A street trader had sold out his entire stock of tomatoes. This was to prove the shortest meeting on record. Though most of the fruit missed me, the crowd's aim being about as accurate as their political knowledge, I thanked them for their attention and declared the meeting closed. "You forgot to take a collection" said the chairman, Jim Kinkaid.

Jim had a dry sense of humour, and you didn't always know whether he was being serious or not, so I just said "bollocks" and retired for a pint.

But back to party life in North West London. I had succeeded in the early thirties in getting, intermittently, work for fairly short periods. The shortest of these was at a factory in Acton Lane called Crypto, which made electrical components. The local party published for this factory a cyclostyled paper which we called *The Fifth Light* (a play on the use by the management of four coloured lights to summon foremen to the office).

A lot of this material was based on information given to us by people working inside. Like most of our industrial activities the paper emphasised the need for trade union organisation and every two weeks or so we would be outside selling it to the workers.

One morning passing the factory, I saw that the 'No' had been removed from the customary 'No hands wanted' which most factories placed outside their premises, so I went in and, to my surprise, was engaged to start the following day.

Reporting for work next morning, I hung about waiting to be shown what to do, when suddenly I was handed an hour's pay and shown the door. Hired, paid and fired all in one hour . . . Not, I'm afraid eligible for the Guinness Book of Records, for this happened all the time to known agitators.

Another place I worked for a while was the Park Royal Coach Works. I was a coach fitter there and had joined the National Union of Vehicle Builders. When we had a dispute, we used to retire to a pub called *The Plumes* to be addressed by a little man with bowler hat and gold watchchain looking like he had stepped right out of one of Low's cartoons. He always made the same speech which was about "how we stood on the stones outside the Chiswick busworks" with little or no reference to the matters that worried us. Years later I heard him make the same speech at Luton when the NUVB were fighting for a foothold at Vauxhall Motors. A nice old chap, but quite clueless in an atmosphere of growing militancy.

I also worked in a rubber factory in the same area and one day was put with another lad to cleaning latex from the inside of a huge metal container using, of all things, benzine.

A young woman who happened to pass by, climbed up onto the staging and seeing two unconscious blokes lying at the bottom, raised the alarm and the next thing we knew we were out in the air being revived. This girl later attempted seduction on the canal bank, and though I tried and tried well; there's gratitude for you.

In the course of party work I'd managed to get arrested a few times and, with one exception, got off with a fine. The exception of which I shall tell later, got me a spell in prison and some years after this I got a job as a fitter in a small factory where a custom-built body was being fabricated to fit a Rolls Royce chassis for a wealthy racing driver. I was told that after two weeks probation I would have a job for life, and so, at seven and a half pence an hour I was getting near to being one of the Labour aristocracy.

Our first child Patricia, had I'm sure, been born and things looked set fair for our little family, until one dinner hour when I had been there about six months we were kicking a ball about in the road outside the factory when a police car went by containing the police inspector who had been the cause of my imprisonment.

The saucy sod had the nerve to nod to me and I thought no more of the incident until at about 4 o'clock the foreman handed me my cards and money telling me I was no longer required. There were no appeal tribunals then, so after repeated unsuccessful attempts to see the boss over a period of several weeks, I gave it up and returned to the dole.

The story of another arrest worth the telling, concerned the public execution of a leading Communist named Edgar Andre.

Hundreds of us lay down in Piccadilly Circus, snarling up the traffic throughout most of the Metropolis. We yelled "Kick Ribbentrop (the Nazi ambassador in London) out of Britain".

At Bow Street next morning, the magistrate asked me if I wanted to start a war and fined me one pound. I pleaded mistaken identity since it was Hitler, not I, who was trying to do just that. So he added another quid onto the fine.

When today's columnists write that the world knew nothing of Nazi atrocities until the Allied troops reached the concentration camps at Belsen and elsewhere in Germany, they either lie or are too lazy to look up the records. I well remember the publication by a broadbased Committee Against War and Fascism, which had some famous names amongst it's sponsors, publishing a book entitled *The Brown Book of Hitler Terror*. I peddled suitcases full of this book, door to door, being most successful in the Jewish district of Brondesbury Park. The book, was documented with supporting photographs of the atrocities even then being committed by the Gestapo against German citizens who opposed their war plans and against those who just happened to be born jewish.

I have today friends whose relatives died in the camps long before Britain declared war on Germany.

I may as well finish the story of my working life (except for Vauxhall, which has a chapter to itself) in case I forget something later.

On returning from Spain, a sympathetic director of a famous chain store had fixed me up with a job with his firm which I had later to decline when the Willesden branch of the Communist Party decided to elect me full-time secretary, a position I held until moving to Hemel Hempstead in September 1939.

Meantime, some comrades in the Electrical Trade Union had managed to get my nomination for membership of that union accepted, and I started work as a wireman's mate with London Transport. The chaps had put me through a week of very rudimentary training in the job, but my shortcomings soon became embarrassingly obvious in this most jealously guarded of trades. An electrician at that time wouldn't even replace a fuse in his own house if someone was watching; so as the few friends I had on the job worked on a different station to me, I was more or less on my own, and after a few months they managed to work me out.

By the early thirties the unemployed had grown to three million. I had been one of them for at least three years, and became a regular speaker at our street corner site near to the Labour Exchange.

Nobody seemed to think it funny that, other speakers being unavailable, I would be called upon by the chairman to make the main speech. Then he would call upon a speaker from the Worker's International Relief (me) then one from the International Labour Defence (me), then someone to appeal for the collection (me again).

So, with all that public speaking experience behind me, I was put up as a supporting speaker to Wal Hannington at a meeting in a local hall. About 600 crowded into the hall, and after questions which brought out a particularly nasty case of the refusal to give food tickets to the family of a bemedalled exserviceman Hannington announced that comrade Horne would tomorrow lead a demonstration to the local Public Assistance Committee to demand justice in this case. (This method of 'election' is known as 'Democratic Centralism').

I think it was New Years Day. The year was 1935. A flurry of snow wafted around the thousand men who waited with a couple of drums and a banner for the meeting to start.

We took the police completely by surprise, so that by the time we reached the PAC offices about a mile away we had only about six policemen with us. Forcing our way into the hall, the delegation first grabbed all the telephones to foil any attempt to get police reinforcements and started to put our case to the Chief Relieving Officer who abruptly turned and left us without a word. We'd forgotten about the telephone in his private room, and in no time at all the hall was full of police who began to arrest members of the deputation while their mounted chums out front beat off the angry crowd.

Attempting to protect my head from the swinging truncheons, I raised a chair over my head. This connected smartly with the nose of the sub-divisional inspector who held me firmly by the collar, causing him to let go with a yell of anguish as he spurted blood in all directions. We arrived at the police station about nine or so in the morning, and I was finally let out on bail at midnight. After dark the cell light went out and I got a hammering from an unknown number of policemen.

Eventually, after several remands I got to the Old Bailey where the court was presided over by the Recorder of London, Sir Ernest Wild, who appeared to sleep soundly throughout the proceedings. I conducted my own defence, a common practice of the Left at that time, to show contempt for class justice and suspicion of the legal profession in general.

In my final appeal to the Jury, in a display of histrionics of which I felt rather proud at the time, I referred to the inscription "engraved on the very walls of this court". This inscription reads, in part – DEFEND THE CHILDREN OF THE POOR – this being the part I had quoted.

After the jury had found me guilty, his Lordship congratulated me on my able defence said, "But you did not complete the quotation, it further says AND PUNISH THE WRONGDOER. That's what I am here for and you will go to prison for six months".

I privately conceded that that had been a rather smart come-back by His Lordship as I made my way down to the cells awaiting the Black Maria that was to take the day's haul to Wormwood Scrubs prison.

Porridge was different then

In the Black Maria, the old lags were handing out advice right and left. "Be a Catholic, you get extra outings for Mass" or "Be a Jew, the food is better and no Saturday work". I took the easy way and opted for Church of England and was thrown a bible and prayer book as we marched through reception.

Later, when I met another 'political' serving twenty months for sedition (giving leaflets to soldiers in Cardiff Barracks) I heard the following story.

Charlie Stead, a South Wales communist, had refused to compromise, proudly declaring his agnosticism. In consequence he was visited nightly for about three weeks by the benign silver-haired Church of England chaplain whose card index doubtless didn't allow for agnostics. Back and forth went the argument until

Harold Horne

Charlie, despairing of ever getting to have a pre-bedtime read, temporised. "Well er' – say I'm a WESLEYAN agnostic' he ventured. The padre trotted away happily and Charles was able to get in some reading.

I remember Charlie with affection and gratitude for his patient explanation of difficult political theory.

We 'in for the causers' were looked upon with amused but pitying tolerance by the criminal element. Homosexuals were derided and made sport of and frequently invited to assignations.Child molesters were often physically attacked. All this despite the fact that no one was supposed to know what you were in for.

I worked in the boiler house, where I sometimes got the unpleasant job of burning the cat 'o nine tails or the birch after a flogging. This was wrapped in a bed sheet and thrown down from the gantry from where the 'screw' was supposed to watch it being burned. If however he turned away, you knew you had to unwrap the ghastly implement so that the screw could take the sheet home.

Not all screws were sadists, so I was unlucky enough to have one on my landing for three of the five months I served. Every single day of those three months I found, on returning to my cell (only one man to a cell then) twice daily, a bucket of cold water and a scrubbing brush, which gave me about one hour to scrub out the cell and all the furniture as well as swallowing the revolting food before returning to work or bedding down for the night.

Two days before my release, he told me that his aim had been to provoke me to violence against his person. I had known this, of course, and always took care to have worked-out of any aggression before the cell door was opened for the morning 'slop out'.

Amongst the people I met in the Scrubs was a prisoner who became nationally known as 'The Officer in the Tower'. Imprisoned for passing military information to the Nazis, he had been an officer of a famous regiment.

Another was an internationally known financier whose depredations had earned him eighteen months, and who would describe in graphic terms the horrific fate awaiting "You lot if you try to start a revolution in England'. I played chess with him at times. Of course he always won.

His cell (kept locked when vacant) was carpeted and book lined.

He had £5 worth of flowers sent in daily and was reputed to have available as much wine and spirits as he could drink.

Once, in the prison hospital with a sprained ankle, I was told I had the signal honour of occupying the cell which 'used to be Lord K . . . 's'. His Lordship, by which title he was always addressed by the screws, had managed to get caught at some financial wizardry concerning a well known shipping line.

On my release I was elected to the Central Committee of the Young Communist League. At my first meeting John Gollan made some critical remarks about the Russian comrades' attempts to interfere in the management of the British YCL. This caused a bit of a rumpus, and later in Moscow I was peripherally involved in discussions about this with, amongst others, Popov and Tanev, co-defendants of George Dimitrov at the Nazi staged trial in Leipzig.

In September of that year (1933) I took part in the unemployed march to the TUC in Brighton, where the General Council succeeded in getting Congress to refuse to see our deputation.

On my release from the Scrubs, I had been given a letter to an employer in Millwall Docks. I opened it of course, throwing it on the fire when I read: "This man is a bit of a tiger, but I know you can tame tigers."

In November 1933 three of us, a Mrs Larkin, Claude Berridge and I contested the Stonebridge Ward in Willesden Urban District Council elections. We got about 1,000 votes each and came close to winning.

They shall not pass

After the elections we turned our attention to the growing menace of fascism represented by Sir Oswald Mosley's British Union of Fascists. As the economic crisis deepened, Mosley's Blackshirts – who affected the SS style uniform familiar to today's TV viewers – stepped up their street violence throughout the country and in particular in the East End of London populated largely by the Jewish poor.

We got a big lift later in 1936 when Mosley, in a much publicised attempt at a provocative march through the Jewish area of

Harold Horne

Whitechapel was prevented from taking a single step by the presence of an estimated one million Londoners who turned up to stop him. Thousands were injured by police batons as they tried to force a way through for Mosley's thugs in fighting that continued the day long, climaxed by the now famous Battle of Cable Street, where the anti-fascists had erected barricades.

Billie, whose courage in these street battles became a byword, once confessed privately to me "The pip-squeaks (her name for the Blackshirts) don't worry me, but those mounted bastards scare the shit out of me". None the less, she was always where the action was.

One time when William Joyce (Lord Haw Haw) was billed to speak in Willesden's Memorial Hall, we decided on a new tactic, and after a sustained press and leaflet campaign we succeeded in effecting a complete public boycott of the meeting.

About a quarter of a mile from the hall was the Jubilee Clock at Harlesden, the traditional meeting place of the area. The Home Secretary had just decreed, in an attempt to minimise the violence at street meetings that a policy of 'first come, first served' was to be enforced by the police.

Now this meeting place was a parking area during the day and therefore unavailable for meetings until 6pm.

The Fascists had kept a guarded platform on the spot all day to be sure of being first. With me hidden in the boot of an old jalopy and grasping a microphone, our old banger turned the corner on the stroke of six. Up I jumped and began to speak, reminding the surprised police and fascists of the Home Secretary's edict. A crowd of about a thousand had gathered whilst back at the hall Joyce addressed a couple of score of the converted.

So they abandoned their meeting and marched over to ours, forcing their way through the crowd and managing to overturn the platform. Joyce got one in the balls from me and a few from others before the mounted police broke up the meeting.

After the War, Joyce was of course, hanged by the British after his trial for treason.

The campaign against fascism in the thirties and forties is now a part of history. Never let it be forgotten; for as Brecht says in the 'The Resistible Rise of Arturo Ui' (Hitler): "The Bitch that spawned him is in heat again."

Harold Horne

The years 1934 and part of 1935 I spent in the Soviet Union about which I write a separate chapter. So we come to mid 1936 when the Spanish generals revolted against their Republican government in an attempt to turn back the clock and return their country to the semi-feudal slavery that it had been until 1931 when the monarchy was ousted.

Many books have been written about the Spanish Civil War, and I believe an authoritative version is presently in production by a former Commander of the British battalion of the International Brigade. (Bill Alexander *British Volunteers for Liberty*.)

In common with most other countries, the movement against war and fascism rallied to the cause of the embattled Republic, demanding the arms denied it under the so-called 'Non Intervention' policy cooked up by Britain and France; while Franco daily received massive supplies of troops and modern weapons from Nazi Germany and Fascist Italy.

So it seemed natural that, after discussing it with Billie, I left her and our then four month old daughter Pat on my way to Spain. The British government had just declared the recruitment of volunteers for Spain to be illegal, so great secrecy was required and steps taken had to be devious and clandestine.

So an August Bank Holiday of 1937 I reported to an address in London where I was given a map of Paris and charged with the responsibility of ensuring the safe arrival in Spain of some twenty other volunteers.

The journey to Paris was fairly uneventful, though there were moments when the lads (most of them on their first foreign trip) tended to bunch around me; the very thing most likely to attract the attention of the sharp-eyed 'flics'. The French underground organisation was superb, and each stage of the journey through France went like clockwork. Until we reached the southern French town of Biarritz.

Up till then I had always spent an hour or so with the guide who was to lead us on the next stage so that we would recognise each other at the next staging post. At Biarritz, however, the police had got wind of our presence and a raid on the hotel where we slept was imminent. Raked from our beds in the early dawn, we climbed through a back window where a fleet of hastily collected cars and taxis waited and in a couple of hours we were in the frontier town of Perpignan where I dispersed the lads in various cafes from which, naturally, some of them gravitated to bordellos.

Making my way to a cafe where I had been told a courier would come for me I sat for an hour or two, lingering as long as possible over my vermouth.As I did not know what this courier looked like I needed to stay sober and alert.

A young Frenchman arrived and a burlesque conversation in broken English and French ensued, all in whispers. My fears about the bona fides of our young friend were somewhat reinforced when in walked an American who had previously met the same young man and, consequently faced the same dilemma.

Eventually after threatening instant death if he proved to be a 'wrong un', we rounded up our lads, all armed with beer bottles as possible weapons and followed the lad down a dark alley to where coaches awaited to take us to the Pyrenean foothills.

On the coach we were issued with rope-soled shoes called *alpagatos*, left the coach and began a twelve hour climb with five minute rests at hourly intervals. We got an extra rest occasionally when we had to lie low at the approach of French mounted patrols.

The sun was high in the heavens when suddenly the guides pointed down to a white house, saying urgently "Casa blanca, Casa blanca, Espana". We ran, rolled and stumbled mercifully downwards to the white house, where, to our profound relief flew the red, gold and purple flag of the Republic.

A few days being counted and recounted in Figueras, and we were taken in trucks on the long journey to Albacete, base of the International Brigades. Driven by American IB veterans we encountered a few road blocks manned by trigger-happy Spaniards who always seemed to want to know more than the Yanks were willing to tell. As a result, the only four words we ever understood of these altercations were "And fuck you too" as gears crashed into first and we moved forward yet again.

It was at Albacete that I first met Will Paynter, who was to become the leader of the South Wales miners; and Andre Marty the French Communist Party leader who first had the idea of an International Brigade to help the Republic.

Eventually we arrived at a small village in the La Mancha

country of Don Quixote which was to be our home for a few weeks whilst we underwent some basic training in modern warfare. Here I was sent to an Officers Training School and promoted to the rank of *sarjento*. One of the lectures was given by Fred Copeman, fresh from a training school on strategy and tactics. Fred, who had been one of the leaders of the 1932 mutiny of the British Atlantic fleet at Invergordon looked, even in his khaki and Sam Browne, every inch a sailor.

The first question came from a Spaniard and concerned some rather complicated calculations of the trajectories of bombs dropped from aircraft. In our OTS we had long theoretical discussions about this and so waited expectantly as the question was translated into English. It became quickly obvious that this had not been one of the subjects included in Fred's curriculum when he fixed the questioner with a baleful stare for five long seconds, and replied dismissively, "Fucked if I know mate, I'm a sailor myself".

Recollection of this incident sparks off memories of others, like Christmas 1937 when the Friends of the Republican Spain in Britain sent parcels to the members of the British battalion. Some of the lads, learning of a proposal to share the Christmas pudding included in each parcel with the Americans, began to bitch. Soon feelings ran sufficiently high to warrant a battalion meeting to debate the issue.

Our Political Commissar, Walter Tapsell, took the rostrum, leading with a ten minute speech on international solidarity and the principles for which we had come to Spain.

Then, suddenly sensing that the slogans were ringing no bells he closed his eyes, spread out his arms, and in a rich fruity Cockney voice declared; "Anyway, anyone who can eat a pahnd 'o pudden is a fucking 'og". Laughter swept the hall, the tension was broken and the Yanks got their share of British Christmas pudding. I reckon there's a lesson there somewhere.

At the training school I had palled up with Leslie Maugham, a grand nephew of the writer Somerset Maugham. Leslie had been a journalist on a local Kettering newspaper, and had hoped to send photographs and reports to his paper from Spain. He was the first man I saw die; killed instantly by a sniper's bullet on the front near the city of Teruel, in mid-sentence as he spoke to me.

Harold Horne

The road from the French frontier to Barcelona runs through the town of Mataro. Briefly hospitalised there following a slight injury incurred in a shooting accident, I often with the other lads would sit outside a certain cafe which sold a tolerable drink euphemistically described as vermouth. From here we could watch the trickle of arms coming from the direction of France. When there would be a break of two or three days in the convoys, we knew that a big offensive was about to be launched somewhere and our 'friends' the Non-Intervention Committee of the League of Nations were at work again, ensuring the Republic was denied the means to defend itself.

One day there walked into this cafe a young man wearing a large Union Jack badge who proved to be some minor bureaucrat from the British consulate in Barcelona. When some of our lads politely asked for news from England, he swore sneeringly making clear in the process his sympathy with Franco. Barring his exit, we discussed loudly whether we should hang or shoot him. White and trembling, he began to plead for British fair play just as a couple of local police arrived to rescue him after he'd shown his diplomatic documents

The policemen joined in our laughter as he stumbled down the steps to his car.

Towards the end of 1938 and shortly before the Spanish Premier Negrin announced to the League of Nations that the demobilisation of the International Brigades had been decided by the Government, I happened to be on leave in Barcelona and staying with a Canadian companion at a small hotel in the city centre. Like all the others, the cuisine consisted exclusively of squid plus, if you had a ration card, which we did, a spoonful of green lentils.

Not really enough for growing lads, so we turned our attention to a British ship which had managed to run the blockade with a cargo of potatoes. The ship had been held up after unloading by some bomb damage and we managed – by a little palm greasing – to get aboard, where the crew greeted us with a huge meal of the kind which we had expected never to see again. This continued for about a week, until the Port Officers caught up with us and sent us off with dire warnings, back to squid and lentils.

However, the night before, the ship's crew presented us each with a sack filled with dried fish, corned beef, canned milk and sugar, and about a million (?) American cigarettes, half of which it cost us to pay off the guards.

The milk, sugar, and some of the meat we distributed to people around the waterfront on a rough and ready system. Milk and sugar to women with small children, corned beef to others who looked hungriest and a handful of fags to old men.

The hotel manager's eyes glowed with avarice when we showed him our haul so we finished up with a sizeable wad of pesetas and he, no doubt, cleaned up by providing these extras to his guest.

I'd read somewhere that in Spain VD was more or less a national pastime, so I had avoided sex for almost a year. However, in Barcelona I formed a brief liaison with a girl whose husband had been killed in the fighting, and spent a reasonably pleasant few weeks with her.

When I showed her pictures of Billie and baby Pat, she cried, saying "Pobrecitos Ingleses" (poor little English) "Their turn next", for no one doubted the truth of La Passionaria's words when she had appealed to the world; "Today it is Madrid, tomorrow it will be Paris and London. Help us."

Because of this success with Rosita, some of my envious mates nicknamed me quite undeservedly, 'Alcalde de Las Ramblas'. The Ramblas in Barcelona is the parade ground for prostitutes.

After demobilisation we were transferred to the small town of Rippol, high in the Pyrenees near the French frontier awaiting repatriation. The British government obstruction which we met at this point is a story in itself.

I was proud though, when reading English newspapers to learn that Billie was playing a leading part in deputations to the Foreign Office in efforts to get the lads home.

Every railway station and even level crossings in France were guarded by steel-helmeted *gardes mobiles* and the train had been routed to avoid Paris.

At Dieppe the whole population seemed to have turned out to greet us – a repeat of the scene at the Spanish frontier town of Puigcerd – which left few dry eyes amongst us.

I forgot to mention that at Ripol when it came my turn to be 'deloused' the machine had run out of steam, so I was reduced to stripping out in the town square at 3am in the freezing mountain air and wiping myself all over with a cloth before donning the trousers and overcoat I'd been given.

This coat, which Billie later dubbed 'The Sleeves' as it seemed to be all sleeves and little else, I wore with a bright green trilby I'd bought in Barcelona. As we arrived at Victoria station, Billie's first words to me were "Blimey, wait till our mum sees that; a proper pox doctor's clerk she'll say".

It seemed that all London had turned out as we tried to march through a cheering throng on our way to the Co-op Hall in Leman Street where a meal was ready for us.

Journey to Moscow

In 1934/5 I spent a year and a half in the Soviet Union. What I saw there exploded forever the old myth that a country could not exist without capitalists.

That is why, despite all that subsequently went wrong and later disillusionment with the Soviet way, I remain to this day a member of the Communist Party of Great Britain.

With two other lads I travelled overland through Belgium, Germany and Poland. Hitler had been in power barely a year and the terror was already well under way.

When our train stopped in the early dawn at Essen in the Ruhr we saw a group of men and women, bloodstained, being beaten with rubber truncheons. As they were urged into trucks, very quickly a line of green uniformed polizei was formed, blocking the scene from the train, on which were many foreigners. As we got further into Germany, one of our number, the youngest – let's call him Tommy – became seized with a missionary zeal directed to the conversion of the most rabid nazis on the train to the principles of Communism. It got quite hairy when an obviously high ranking nazi in Goering style uniform boarded the train at the Alexanderplatz station in Berlin. Tommy went for him hammer and sickle, especially when he gave a plug for Oswald Mosley and his Blackshirts who were to bring 'order' to decadent Britain. He almost had apoplexy when Tommy drew his attention to some Communist wall slogans, and spluttered threats of the fate that awaited Jews and Communists in

Hitler's 'New Order'. After the nazi had left the train, we gave Tommy a 'going over, pointing out that we were supposed to be non-political tourists; our passports were being examined every few miles and we were questioned on the purpose of our visit and of our ultimate destination which we had said was Warsaw.

I'm sure that only our British passports saved us from arrest because at that time Hitler was anxious to present a reasonable and civilised image to the world. We'd heard of more than one foreign traveller through Germany who had ended up in a Nazi gaol.

Nowhere could we find the cushions for hire which, we had been told, were available for use on the hard slatted wooden seats of the train. We did manage to get some soup and oranges, and in Poland, some black bread and garlic sausage which nigh destroyed our taste buds for ever.

So our train crawled into no-mans land, where we transferred to the wider-gauged Russian train for the few yard's journey to the actual frontier station of Negoralyie in the Union of Soviet Socialist Republics.

In the land of the Soviets

Welcome to the Workers of the World proclaimed the multi-lingual streamer spread across the huge arch which straddled the rail tracks at the Soviet frontier.

At last, after a three day journey, we were home in the workers' fatherland. I thought of the American John Reed who said "I've seen the future, and it works", and of Wal Hannington on a visit to Moscow who said to his fellow tourists; "Look lads, and it's all ours".

Now we had soft seats and sleeping compartments, and hot meals with piles of delicious Ukrainian wheat bread. Awaking in the morning with the grinding of brakes, we got our first shock.

The train and platform swarmed with beggars, mostly children, the so called *besprizorni* (homeless children) the terrible legacy of the Civil War and the Wars of Intervention.

We knew enough not to expect milk and honey just yet, but when some English-speaking Russian told us that these were 'speculators' we smiled politely, for none were wearing the bowler hats and spats favoured by the speculators to whom we were accustomed.

Rome wasn't built in a day, and it was, after all, a mere year or two since the Red Army had driven the capitalist "pigs' snouts from the Soviet garden".

In Moscow we did the obligatory round of rubbernecking, standing in the never-ending queue to see the body of Lenin in his glass coffin centred in the impressive red marble mausoleum against the Kremlin wall and visiting the huge GUM department store, where the sales system seemed specially designed to inhibit would-be purchasers.

Visiting the great coal mining complex at Tula near Moscow we were given gargantuan meals of fried pork, potatoes and onions, (the Russian are great trenchermen). Trouble was, the menu was the same at every meal; breakfast, lunch, tea, first supper, and then second supper. This went on for a whole week.

In the summer, on a visit to the beautiful city of Kharkhov in the Ukraine, we went to collective farms where wheat and melons were cultivated in areas as big as Yorkshire and in some cases bigger.

It was in Kharkhov that with one of the lads who had travelled with me through Germany (not Tommy), we met a couple of girls who invited us to their one room flat "To play chess".

I soon learned how to mate in one and a good time was had by all, until early one morning we crept back to our digs. While climbing through the window we were fired at by a militiaman, as Soviet policemen are called. Surviving that by climbing fully dressed into bed and closing our eyes tightly whilst an hour long search of the premises was conducted we returned to Moscow.

Back in the capital, the more decadent amongst the foreign colony scorned the official ski-ing and other sport fanatics and diverted ourselves with parties, drink, food and fruit obtained from the 'Torgsin'"store which only took foreign money or precious metals. When we ran out of foreign cash we sometimes took a gold watch. The girl at the cash desk would rip out the works, weigh the gold and hand over what seemed like a million roubles. This would be enough to keep us going for weeks with drink and stuff unobtainable in normal shops.

Other times we went to a night club which we called the Bucket of Blood. This usually ended with our having to make long speeches of 'self criticism' before our peers with promises not to offend again as these places we were told were the haunts of spies and other imperialist agents.

The only ones who never came to the Bucket of Blood were the Germans, of whom there were about thirty in the foreign colony at the time. We learned why later, when on return to their homeland the whole lot were arrested at the frontier (despite having split up and travelling at different times to avoid detection) and tortured to death by the nazis.

One day we paid a visit to the Kremlin to meet Krupskaya, the widow of Lenin. This frail-looking, white-haired old lady who looked as if she might have just come from the vicar's tea party, treated us to a little homily on political morality and the need for honesty and decency in human relations. It was so nice, and I have never forgotten her words which, in the light of Kruschev's later revelations about the Stalin era I'm sure held a greater significance than any of us realised at the time.

On 1 December 1934 the leader of the Leningrad Soviet and Party Sergei Kirov was assassinated in his office. We marched in the funeral parade through the Red Square crying with the marching millions "Death to the traitorous agents of foreign imperialism" And a darkness fell over the land which lasted until the Khruschev revelations in 1956.

It would take a whole book to tell of my sojourn in the land of socialism. Let me just end this chapter on a slightly lighter note.

Anniversary day of the 1917 Revolution is 7 November. On that day in 1934 I was yanked from my bed at 5am (and it can be bloody cold in Moscow in November) by a cheer leader with cries of "Its Revolution Day".

Indiscreetly I countered with "Fuck the Revolution" before wriggling back under the blankets.

By the time I had finished my self criticism I was knee deep in my own gore, and sure that I was on my way to Siberia.

Miraculously, I survived as you see.

Billie

Before going to prison I had been paying court to a young woman – a friend of Billie. Billie began to 'go steady' with Harry – my old school chum who appears elsewhere in this story – a real *Girls Own Paper* scenario. When I was sentenced this girl's father had, very properly, warned her of the consequences of continued association with 'that gaolbird', a warning she chose to ignore at the time and thus she wrote to me in prison.

In my starry-eyed reply, so help me, I had quoted a bit from Omar Khayam:

"Ah love, could thou and I with fate conspire
To change this sorry scheme of things entire
Would we not shatter it to bits and then
Remould it nearer to the hearts desire"

Have a good laugh on me. I swear to you that it didn't seem at all funny at the time; at least not to me. I found out on my release that this girl had fallen about laughing, as had the girls in her office to whom she had shown the letter. I was furious of course and broke off the affair at once.

About this time we had embarked on a 'chalking' campaign against fascism and unemployment and practically every unmarked wall in Willesden got the treatment of our whitewash brushes. Billie and I were always heavily involved in this activity which gradually became an essential part of our subsequent courtship. She was always a smartly dressed girl, and tended to wear high heeled shoes, the higher the better. Though I had a thing about 'killer dillers' (and still have) I would not at that time have admitted it for all the tea in China. In later years she liked to entertain friends with the story of how on one chalking foray her five-inch heel had broken off and she had to be taken home hopping on one foot and being denounced by me as 'petty bourgeois.'

When I got her to her home I surprised myself by making what for me amounted to a proposal of marriage. She replied with "I'm like the Mounties, I always get my man".

For a short time we did our chalking in style using a car, complete with chauffeur, belonging to the father of one of the YCLers. This young lad, who is now a wealthy business man, would

AEU Luton District Committee at the opening of their new office 1 April 1970. Guest speaker was the recently elected president Hugh Scanlon. *Fourth from the left front row.* Harold Horne *standing behind Scanlon.* Owen Hardisty *tallest in the back row.* **PHOTO** *Luton News*

First meeting of the Vauxhall Shop Stewards Combine Committee 1965 Swan Hotel Brownhills Staffordshire 1965 Harold Horne third from left

load up the car with buckets of whitewash and brushes and order Johnson (who was a loyal ex-Bengal Lancer and hated our guts). "Stop at this corner Johnson" and out we'd get, do our stuff and back in the car for the next blank wall.

On the 28 September1935 we took a couple of hours off from the revolution to get married at Willesden Registry Office and, to the disgust of our respective mothers, (the only guests) went straight out to sell *The Young Worker* in Kilburn High Road.

Thus began a wonderful relationship which lasted until Billie's death on 29 January 1978.

Amy Yates, known from childhood as Billie was born in Lambeth on 8 April 1916. Moving to Willesden with her widowed mother in 1926 she entered St Mary's Girls School and, says her school leaving report, became "top girl of the school".

When we moved to Luton in 1940 she took up Party work with renewed vigour, eventually becoming a full-time worker at the office of the South East Midlands District of the Communist Party and sat on a number of National Women's committees. She served as a district committee and secretariat member for some years and worked tirelessly in the great war time campaigns for the opening of the Second Front and the defeat of Nazism.

Vivacious and fun loving, at a time when fun was not too highly regarded as a useful attribute to party work, she had also a caustic wit which she used to good purpose to deflate the pompous and occasionally to bring a meeting back to reality; earning for herself the sobriquet 'down to earth Billie'.

In 1938 she organised and led what I believe was the first school strike in Britain for safety measures to be taken on a dangerous road. This won national press recognition and was completely successful.

In her middle fifties she achieved her 'O' levels in English literature, a fact of which she was justly proud.

In October 1970 at an event in Luton Town Hall to celebrate the 50th anniversary of the Communist Party, Billie received from Peter Kerrigan on behalf of the Party, a certificate commemorating her 37 years membership, making her, I believe, the second longest serving member in the district at that time.

Although acidly condemnatory when the occasion demand, she

had a deep underlying compassion for human weakness.

Back in our Willesden days an old chap (allegedly attracted to small boys) had climbed the five flights to our two-roomed flat looking starved and ill. Billie gave him the only food in the house, half a dozen buns left over from Easter. He wolfed the lot, thanked us and left.

A week later we went to his funeral, the only mourners; "Poor old sod" she said, "At least he had someone to see him off".

She would never pass a street singer without tossing a coin into the cap or tin cup, or if without money, making a mental note to pay double next time. Except for her last illness, and a war time period in hospital with near fatal meningitis, she never took to her bed when unwell. "Get up and work it off" she would say, it soon goes". All her days a fighter was Billie.

Let Owen Hardisty, whose friendship with that of his wife Maureen we have cherished since the early forties, finish the story. In a tribute at her funeral he said;

"Widely read and articulate, she could more than hold her own with the best. "

To her family, friends and neighbours she was a tower of strength in time of trouble, dispensing practical help and comfort with natural generosity and a 'never say die' brand of earthy humour which uplifted every one around her.

In any assessment of the life of Billie Horne, the theme of concern for humanity recurs again and again.

> Confronted with oppression she stood for Liberty.
> Confronted with War she stood for Peace.
> Confronted with racial hatred she stood for the Brotherhood of Man.

One cannot forsee in detail what the future holds for our people, but of this I am confident – It will, and indeed must be, a society based on the principles she upheld. For the Billie Hornes of this world are invincible".

Harold Horne

Our family

We had four children who in turn presented us with twelve grand children.

Our first, Patricia was born 17 March 1937 and was four months old when I left for Spain, became a school teacher and now lives in Leeds. She has two sons and a daughter and organises charitable works and broadly-based protest movements against such things as proposed motorways, airport expansions and the like.

Peter was born in Hemel Hempstead on 21 October 1939. He served two years in the Parachute Regiment and is now a Community Recreation Officer operating in the big council estate at Farley Hill Luton. He has two sons.

Jill, who despite her five children (three boys two girls) is perhaps the most politically committed being an active Labour Party member. She was born on 28 December 1943.

Ted the youngest born 16 March 1946 is now a planning engineer at Vauxhall Motors. We took some pride in the fact that, as he once told us, he is often asked questions by men twice his age about politics and unions, questions he could have answered at the age of twelve. He has one son and a daughter.

Though none of them has followed us all the way politically, they are each in their own way socially-oriented.

If we had any regrets at all, it was perhaps that our political preoccupations allowed us less time with the children than we would have wished, though they were by no means neglected.

We consoled ourselves with the thought that we were after all helping to build a better life for them. For we had, and I still have ,the conviction with Robbie Burns:

> "It's coming yet for a' that
> That man to man the warld o'er
> Shall brithers be for a' that"

However that may be, our children have, despite some set-backs and disappointments, given us a lifetime of happiness, and since the death of their mother, have saved me from the totality of despair.

After the war we managed a few camping holidays at Clacton or on the river Ouse at Bedford which helped to make up for the heartaches which went with the times of poverty and wartime shortages.

I remember well the tears that came as I fitted three year old Pat with her Mickey Mouse gas mask, and Billie placed baby Peter in the plastic fronted container with hand-operated pump, which was supposed to protect children from enemy gas attack.

And the dark unspoken thoughts that came one night as we looked at the sleeping children after we'd been woken by bells ringing (church bells were to be rung in the event of invasion) and the sound of marching feet in the street outside.

It turned out to be fire engines in the Hitchin road on their way to just-blitzed Coventry and the local Home Guard doing a night exercise.

These thoughts were to return when some fifteen years later we stood on the terraces of the great Nazi built stadium in Nuremburg where the 'laws' on The Final Solution of the Jewish Problem were proclaimed.

Vauxhall – the Skipper and me

It was sometime during the last quarter of 1939 that we moved to Hemel Hempstead to live with my sister Jess and her husband. This was to have been a temporary arrangement so that Billle could have the baby she was expecting in the quiet atmosphere of the Hertfordshire countryside. Hemel was then just a largish village with little industry apart from the paper mills of John Dickenson.

I was still with London Transport and would get up at 5am to cycle to Watford where I got the train to Baker Street. However, my shortcomings as an electrician were becoming increasingly apparent and I could sense the increasing hostility of my fellow workers and soon I was back on the dole. I used to cycle around Hemel and the surrounding area in search of the non-existent work.

In September Hitler invaded Poland and Britain had been forced to declare war on Germany. On 21 October our second child Peter was born, and so, when someone suggested I try for work at the Vauxhall Motors factory at Luton, I did so and used to travel by train on a little-used branch line and three buses to get there.

Harold Horne

When I first set eyes on the great industrial complex that was Vauxhall my heart sank into my shoes. They would surely have a blacklist and I would be known to them. They had a list all right but my fame had not yet reached this far north and this industry. I got the job by inventing fictitious jobs to cover my unemployed periods in London industry and my spell in the Scrubs. I nearly slipped up when the Employment Manager questioned me closely about one of my fairy tales which covered a part of Willesden with which he was well acquainted. Years later, when I had achieved some prominence and a goodly backing amongst the workers, my little deception became a bit of a standing joke in management circles.

After my first spell on nightwork (month about) I announced to Billie that I'd give it another fortnight and then back to London. Nearly thirty two years later I retired from Vauxhall on health grounds at the age of sixty one.

My first act on moving to Luton in March 1940 was to rejoin the AEU and gradually made contact with the few party members working at the factory. Owen Hardisty was an apprentice at the time and became politically involved a little later.

My first meeting with Vauxhall Communists nearly drove me bonkers. A consequence of the Soviet/German non-aggression pact was that the press had labelled us 'Communazis' and I found the group preparing for illegality and working out a complicated system of inter-departmental communication. When at last we managed to convince the lads that going underground was no answer we began to work on the problem of trade union organisation which was then almost non-existent.

The firm's managing director Mr (later knighted) Charles Bartlett was paternalistic to a degree and known to view unionism in his factory with disfavour. So it was an uphill battle especially as wages were always just that little bit higher than elsewhere.

At the turn of the century local authorities were advertising in London and Midland papers to attract industry to their town with inducements like low rates, cheap land, where 'Labour is docile" (the actual words) and trade unions "Virtually non-existent".

So in 1905 the Vauxhall Iron Works in the Vauxhall district of London – where two years earlier the first Vauxhall car had been built – moved to Luton and was taken over twenty years later by the giant American General Motors Corporation.

CJB, as Bartlett was known in the works, displayed to my mind some evidence of delusions of grandeur and built around himself a management team each of which reported directly to him. This helped him in restraining the more brash labour policies of his US bosses and indicated his political foresight of the shape of things to come on the labour front.

Ford had barely got going at Dagenham, so the only competition came from a multiplicity of small firms like Morris, Austin, Standard and Rootes. If anything, Vauxhall tended to get the lions share of Government contracts with it's famous Bedford trucks and, later the Churchill tank.

A rather complicated group bonus scheme was operated which was a constant source of conflict – unfortunately more often between individuals and groups of workers than with the company. I often wondered why they bothered with foremen since each man became, under the bonus system, the slave driver to his fellow workers.

When, years later we negotiated out of the bonus system and onto measured day work, it became fashionable in some circles to attack this move on the grounds that we had sold out too cheaply. I tried to get a meeting with fellow convenors in the Midlands. I met only derision for their piecework earnings were beginning to outstrip Vauxhall. The lads would point to Ford who had never had payment by results and whose wages were at the bottom of the wages league. I think that today the evils of PBR are widely recognised and the advantages of plain time payment in terms of growing national unity of car workers is obvious.

In 1945 I was elected shop steward in the rear axle shop which included the heat treatment of differential gears. This work was heavy, hot and dirty, and the men's tally of the weekly output rarely agreed with that of the supervision so that each Thursday when bonus figures were published I invariably found myself in the office arguing the case. On one such occasion the area manager took me by the arm, and led me into the heat treatment area where sat all the lads having an extended tea break and playing with an improvised ouija board. A few were hanging out washing alongside the furnaces.

Remarking "That's where the bonus went" George (the manager) returned with me to the office where sat some grinning foremen. Feeling that some comment was needed I said: "Alright for you George. Sitting there while we sweat our balls off".

Looking at me over the top of his spectacles he replied; "Anytime your balls sweat, bring em in and lay 'em on this desk". Turning abruptly I left, slamming the door with such force that the glass panel shattered. We got on famously after that.

Parallel with trade union work, the party branch began to hold regular lunchtime meetings on the canteen steps at which I was usually the main speaker. At one such during the war we had distributed a leaflet which called for the setting up of a joint production committee. Mr Bartlett on his way to lunch had taken one of the leaflets and turning to his companion said; "There you are, that's what we want". A few weeks later the setting up of a committee was announced which became known as the Management Advisory Committee.

After the war, this committee (MAC) on which I sat for some twenty five years with ever increasing majorities at each election, had as it's main objective the isolation of the unions and the instilling of a 'one happy family' atmosphere in the works.

Over the years those with longer vision resisted the demands of a small but vociferous minority to 'Smash the MAC' – realising that it had widespread support on the shop floor and that withdrawal would, in fact, bring about the very isolation we worked to avoid.

It took about out a quarter of a century to get full trade union recognition at Vauxhall and those who had patiently and skilfully used the MAC to this end had cause to celebrate when at long last the MAC died and trade unionism came into it's own.

In 1945 Vauxhall's first strike occurred in the body shop over bonus earnings on the new peacetime car which was just beginning to come into production. It lasted a few days and succeeded completely in achieving our demands, but from then on I and a few other militants became marked men so far as the management was concerned. But a big growth in union membership had resulted.

At this time and for many years after, it was common practice for management to go over the heads of shop stewards and do telephone deals with union officials, often from Head Office, and in consequence, we faced for some years the humiliation of minimal wage offers being thrown at us with 'take it or leave it' attitude. Of course management was not without collaborators in the trade union field. Together they spent an awful lot of time in attempting to clobber us, but we quickly learned the 'softly softly' approach, always making sure that we kept in touch with, and reflected, shop floor aspirations.

I suppose about a dozen or more *coups d'etat* were set up to entrap me and I won't bore the reader with all of them. Some however are interesting, and in some ways laughable.

In 1951 a so-called New Wage Structure was proposed by management and a ballot form was printed for workers to vote on one of three alternatives, A fourth alternative proposed by us did not appear on the ballot paper. The ballot was to be conducted by the MAC so I threw the shit in the fan by collecting all the unmarked ballots in my constituency (about one thousand) and returned them to the MAC secretary who asked innocently, "What am I going to do with these?" I gave the classic reply and left his office.

A couple of days later I was summoned to Bartlett's office. The whole plant waited for the outcome, it being widely believed that I was at last for the high jump. I knew, however, that if I was sacked a large part of the factory would stop work and this helped me a lot in the eyeball to eyeball confrontation.

CJB was a self made man. He had started at Vauxhall as a stores clerk and worked his way to top man. Like many of his kind he appeared to be enamoured of the ideas of corporativsm and the 'leader principle'. When he was later knighted he caused to have issued a letter to all employees headed "Think of me simply as the Skipper").

Anyway, at that meeting I was to see another 'old man' to that which his employees knew. Starting off with threats of dismissal if I continued to rock the boat he went into a long discourse of what he was trying to do at Vauxhall, taking as he said, "The best out of Communism and the best from Capitalism" and how this could become a unifying factor throughout the nation. A bit of philosophy and a tour of Russia, China and the United States, ending with a job offer if I played ball and a hard bed if I didn't.

Harold Horne

He also quoted from the court scene of *The Merchant of Venice* as a lead-in to one of the most virulent anti-semitic tirades I had ever heard. I realise that unless this interview was taped, (which it may well have been) I have no proof of all this, but every word is the naked truth and I would be prepared to swear before any court as to it's veracity.

Years later when the Tavistock Institute of Human Relations or some such body did one of the then-fashionable surveys of labour attitudes, I mentioned to a woman member of the investigating body whom I knew slightly, that CJB was, in my opinion, extremely right-wing politically and hankered for the Corporate State on Mussolini lines. She thought I was exaggerating, until after a talk with him she did confess to me that she agreed mainly with what I had said.

Despite all this, I could still feel sorry for him when General Motors moved in the heavy gang and deposed him. Many of those he had promoted to management deserted him fearful of their jobs under the new regime.

He died soon after, and at his funeral in Luton's St Mary's church I experienced a genuine sorrow that one of my class (for such he had been once) should end up thus.

On another occasion, some company official whom I won't name, thought he had detected an attempt by me to overclaim on my MAC expenses and forthwith involved other management people in what was to be 'Harold Horne's Swan Song'. This affair ended in ignominy for my accusers.

In 1967 a strike took place at the Luton and Dunstable factories over the refusal by management to meet our full wage demands – (I had by then become the union convenor at the Dunstable plant). This lasted a week by the end of which we had discovered that the Ellesmere Port plant had not supported us due to weak leadership, and when the company said they would open the plants on the following Monday and unlimited overtime would be available, the strike began to break. A last minute involvement of the Buckinghamshire MP Robert Maxwell failed to alter the company's stand, merely providing a formula for a return to work on company terms. We had to call it a day. In consequence there are those who still today think we 'sold them down the river' not realising that

Harold Horne

leadership means more than calling the troops into action. I believe
that the expression 'too many chiefs and not enough redskins'
originated with that episode.

The inner-union battle for leadership, usually referred to as the
Left/Right struggle, sometimes had it's funny moments – like the
occasion when the shop stewards secretary had broken his pencil
point and asked "Anyone got a knife?". Quick as a flash came the
answer from Glyn Morgan (the present Luton plant convenor),
"Take one from Harold's back".

In 1958 I attended a Conference in Rome organised by the Italian
Communist Party on the subject of the 'Tactic of Human Relations
in Industry'.

Delegates from all over Europe, the USA and Canada attended
and I learned much that helped me in the battle against class
collaboration at Vauxhall. Looking at today's political scene there is
still a long way to go.

At the end of 1971 I retired from Vauxhall on health grounds at
the age of 61.

I take pride in the fact that I received tributes and presentations
from all sections of the trade union movement as well as the shop
floor whom I'd tried to battle for over some 32 years. I had at least
earned the respect, if not the support, of political enemies and
management too.

I am typing this story on the desk presented to me by Dunstable
plant shop stewards.

Modern Times

If you saw the film starring Charlie Chaplin called *Modern Times*
you will have laughed at the scene where Charlie leaving the works
is walking along the street, his hands still making the motions that
they have been doing in the factory all day. Not so much an
exaggeration as you might think. During your daily or nightly stint
you are living two lives. While your hands automatically perform
the monotonously repetitive motions, your mind is back home in
bed with the wife, doing your fretwork, winning the hundred yard
sprint, catching a record fish, or whatever turns you on.

Inevitably accidents happened. One man who worked on a grinding machine would occasionally, (usually at the same time in the morning) lean a bit too heavily on the feed wheel and a half hundred weight of steel with chunks of carborundum would fly like shell fire about the shop. Everyone ducked; everyone that is except this operator, who always tried to catch the heavy axle tube in mid air. I think he got three broken arms before they moved him to a less hazardous job.

I happened one night to hear the lads talking about D who nightly did ten extra jobs "For the war effort".

Concealing myself behind a pillar I watched at the end of the shift as this man continued the motions of machining the imaginary component ten times before cleaning down the machine. This continued throughout the war. After the 'ten extra' he would walk around the outside perimeter of the building (about half a mile) back to the wash room a few yards from his machine, wash his hands and another half mile back to his machine to await the knocking off hooter.

Another man would start his machine, lean on a pillar and sleep for the six minutes it took the machine to complete the operation. Nothing could wake him until the end of the six minutes, when he would change the component and then back to sleep.

There was also a man who wandered from shop to shop (Vauxhall is housed in many separate buildings) to stand behind an operator miming the man's movements. When challenged he would declare that this job was rightfully his. One day he was taken off to the mental hospital at Arlesey which held a goodly number of Vauxhall workers amongst it's patients. No compensation is as yet paid for injury to the mind.

Trades unions in Luton

In 1940 I had joined Luton No. 8 branch of the AEU and sometime later with a few other members of the branch we formed a new branch known as Round Green. This was the beginning of a rapid growth of new AEU branches in the town and I was later elected as a delegate to the Trades Council.

The Trades Council had done sterling work at the turn of the century in trying to organise the workers in the town (mostly hat workers) into unions, but this had been an uphill battle as many workers failed to see the relevance of trade unions in the relatively prosperous town in which they worked.

Old Luton trades unionists have told me that a less than warm welcome was extended to the 1932 Hunger Marchers when they passed through the town on their way to London.

However, during and just after the war the Trades Council revived and began to play a more significant part in the town's affairs and the activities of the trade union movement generally.

I recall the arrival at the Trades Council meetings of a delegate from the Transport Workers' Union. He attended perhaps six meetings, always stood at the back and seized every opportunity to make anti-Communist speeches. He was merely establishing his credentials for inclusion on Labour's parliamentary panel. He became subsequently a minister in the Labour government. His name was George Brown.

I became successively, president of Round Green AEU district committee delegate representing the AEU shop stewards, acting president of the district committee and a delegate to the regional committee.

Among my proudest possessions is the AUEW Award of Merit which I received from executive council in 1970.

Shop window to the west

Early on in the war years after we had come to Luton, we became friendly with a couple of Oxford graduates, Lionel and Lucy Munby, who lived in a village a few miles from Cambridge. We spent many pleasant holiday week-ends in their lovely old house, and Billie officiated at the birth of two of their three children.

It was through their generosity that we were able to holiday twice in Czechoslovakia, first in 1961 together with the Munby family and our youngest son Ted, and again in 1964 when Billie and I went alone.

Our hosts in Prague were the Teich family, a couple with two

Harold Horne

children, with whom we became and remained firm friends.

We were excited by the prospect of seeing at first hand a country that we all looked upon as Communism's shop window to the West. The most technically advanced and, we believed, the most democratic in form of the Eastern European countries we hoped that Czechoslovakia would be able to show us a glimpse of the "Socialism with a human face" for which we longed after the trauma of the events in Hungary which Billie had visited in 1959.

We travelled overland by car and camped *en route*. On the first visit the most notable stopping place was Nuremburg in Western Germany. Here a big international camping site has been constructed close to the gigantic nazi-built stadium where the laws on the Final Solution to the Jewish Problem were first promulgated.

Standing on the now overgrown terraces, we fancied we could hear the echos of the 'Seig Heils' that had some fifteen years before greeted Hitler and his evil genius Goebbels and we reflected on how close indeed we ourselves and our own country had come to disaster.

When right after this somewhat emotional experience we entered a church of mediaeval origin, I watched Billie out of the corner of my eye as the cleric in charge traced his church's history with the aid of illustrations pinned to the wall. I saw she was becoming more and more angry as he came to the war period. When he began to describe some damage done to the church by Allied bombs as a 'war crime' she interjected with; "And have you seen what your bombers did to Coventry Cathedral?" turned and stalked out fuming with rage.

In the beautiful and historic city of Prague we got a few shocks. We met many interesting people and burned the midnight oil in discussions where we learned, aided by what we ourselves observed, that all was not well with the economy and that there existed many restrictions on personal freedom that we had hoped had gone with the passing of the Stalin era.

Whenever we stopped in Prague's centre we were at once surrounded by crowds of curious people who would examine our cars, a mini and a dormobile caravan with great interest. In the course of the impromptu discussions thus engendered we learned of

Harold Horne

many shortages of consumer goods and lack of services due to bureaucratic over centralisation.

One such we ourselves experienced when a window in our host's house was broken. When I offered to repair the window I was told that this was not possible since glass and putty could not be bought and glaziers as we know them are non existent. So we had to take out the whole frame and pay three visits to a glazier to get the repair done. It had it's funny side on holiday in midsummer. Less funny though in winter struggling to get your window frame onto a tram car you can imagine.

When we invited people to visit us if ever they came to England we were told that whole families were never allowed to leave the country. Always at least one member had to remain to guarantee the family's return.

On our second visit in 1964 we travelled widely through the country and I got in some fabulous fishing in the great lakes near Czeske Budjovice not far from the Austrian border.

Billie was moved to tears when we were told that the grassy slope on which we walked one day had once been the main street of the village of Lidice, where the entire village had been wiped off the map by the Nazis. All the adults were shot and the children shipped to Germany as slave labour in reprisal for the assassination of Gauleiter Heydrich by the resistance.

Back in Luton in 1968 we were elated when we heard the news of the so-called 'Prague Spring' which, led by Alexander Dubcek had brought about a change of leadership with a promise of reforms based on a policy of 'socialism with a human face'.

When later the armies of the Warsaw Pact invaded Czechoslovakia we did for the first time seriously consider our continued membership of the party.

To its everlasting credit, the congress of the British party overwhelmingly condemned the invasion and has continued to protest the presence of foreign troops in that country.

In the days before Kruschev's revelations of the crimes committed in Russia during Stalin's reign, there used to be a huge statue of the Russian leader dominating the centre of Prague and facing the football ground. A joke told at the time was, "Now they daren't lose".

Harold Horne
biographical details

1911   Born at Willesden 1911. One of four sons and three daughters, the survivors of tne ten children of George William Henry Horne a labourer.

1930   Joined the Communist Party. Unemployed in the great depression of the 1930s he became a leading activist in the Willesden National Unemployed Workers Movement (NUWM)

1933   Led a demonstration to the Public Assistance Committee, tried at the Old Bailey and jailed for six months. Elected to the Central Committee of the Young Communist League. Organised and led many demonstrations against Mosley's blackshirts.

November 1933 Contested Stonebridge ward in Willesden Urban District Council elections.

1934   Until mid-1935 studied at the Moscow Lenin School.

August 1937 Joined the International Brigade of the Spanish Republican Army. Involved in many of the most bitterly fought battles, twice wounded and promoted to Company Commander.

November/December 1938 Repatriated to England.

1939   Found work at the Vauxhall Motors Luton.

1942   Communist Party at Vauxhall agitated for joint production committees to assist the War effort. Harold was elected to Vauxhall's first Management Advisory Committee.

1943   Elected AEU shop steward.

1945   Led Vauxhall's first strike to a successful end.

1963   Elected Convenor of shop stewards at the Bedford truck plant at Dunstable, successively president of Round Green AEU branch; district committee delegate representing Luton shop stewards; acting president of the AEU district committee; delegate to the AEU regional committee.

1970   Received the AUEW Award of Merit from the executive council.

1971   Retired from Vauxhall Motors due to failing health.

November 1978   Died at home shortly after completing his biography *'All The Trees Were Bread and Cheese'*.

1979   Harold Horne Memorial Fund established by Dunstable Truck plant shop stewards.

Billie Horne

8 April 1916   Born in Pimlico Road Lambeth. The daughter of William Frederick Yates Private 22nd Royal Fusiliers (deceased) and Amy Elizabeth Yates, registered name Amy Muriel Mary but always known as 'Billie'. Her great uncle was Harry Castling the composer of the famous music hall songs 'Just like the Ivy', 'Let's all go down the Strand' and others.

1926   Moved to Willesden with her widowed mother and attended St. Mary's Girls School.

1932   Joined the Young Communist League and met Harold Horne. Organised sleeping accommodation, food distribution and meeting halls when Willesden hosted the Scottish hunger marchers participating in the great march on Parliament.

1933/1935   Played a prominent role in the NUWM campaigns organised under the slogan; 'WE REFUSE TO STARVE IN SILENCE' as a propagandist and agitator. Along with Harold she became courageous demonstrator and street fighter in opposing Mosley's British Union of Fascists.

26 September1935 Married Harold Horne at Willesden Register Office shortly after his return from Moscow.

17 March 1937 First child Patricia was born, just four months before Harold left to fight in Spain.

1938 Organised the first school strike in Britain to enforce safety measures on a dangerous road.

1939 Moved to Luton .

1942/1945 Involved in many wartime campaigns for munitions production and the opening of the Second Front. Served, as a member of the district committee of the SE Midland's Communist Party and the National Womens committee.

1946 The family now comprised: Patricia born1937, Peter born 1939, Jill born 1945 and Ted born 1946.

1960 Became a full time worker at the SE Midlands distict Communist Party office. Actively involved in the peace movement and local politics.

1970 On the 50th anniversary of the Communist Party presented with a certificate marking her 37 years membership.

January 1978 Died at Luton.

Memorial tribute to Harold Horne

Given at his funeral by Owen Hardisty

"Friends, here at the end of a life devoted to the service of the
Labour movement lies our dear friend and comrade Harold
Horne.

To Pat, Ted, Peter, Jill and all his family we extend our
deepest sympathy. They know that we, his friends, share their
sense of great personal loss.

We mourn the passing of one known for his magnificent
fighting spirit and puckish humour, loved for his warmth and
humanity and respected by his adversaries for his honesty and
courage.

It is hard to realise that we will not see Harold again; that
his invaluable help and inspiring leadership will be gone from
amongst us.

None will miss him more than his workmates and trade
union brothers at the Vauxhall plants where for so many years
he devoted his great talents to the welfare of his mates and the
building of the trade unions.

When Harold came to Luton and started work at the
Vauxhall plant 39 years ago, union membership was almost
non-existent: and certainly so in the production areas where he
worked. Along with such stalwarts as Alec Tuckwell, Tom Adair
and the late Jim Kinkaid, he worked ceaselessly to build the
AEU and together with them represented his members'
interests on the Management Advisory Committee from it's
inception in 1942.

In that year also he became a founder member of the Round
Green branch of the AEU whose chairman he ultimately
became, and of which he remained a member until his death.

On his transfer to the Dunstable truck plant, he continued
his work as a shop steward and was repeatedly elected by the
Luton area stewards to represent them on the union's district
committee on which he served for many years. His qualities of

Harold Horne

leadership were recognised by the Dunstable plant stewards who elected him their first convenor, a position he held until his retirement in 1971.

Today no one doubts that the strength and vigour of the trade unions within the plants owes much to the many years of hard work, the tenacity and courage of Harold Horne. Even after his retirement he retained close links with the Trade Union movement and was elected AEU district referee.

But no mere record of events can explain the trust placed in him and the affection in which he was held. To anyone affected with doubt or despair he was the breath of life, encouraging, guiding and giving practical help with a natural generosity.

Whenever the going got tough, as in the late forties and early fifties Harold was seen at his best. This was the zenith of the cold war when all the might of the establishment and the media was turned against the left.

How well we recall Harold addressing hostile meetings at the factory gate, and week after week parrying hecklers with his devastating wit and unshakable logic until even his bitterest opponents were outspoken in admiration of his courage.

It was this quality, together with his obvious sincerity and integrity which persuaded even those who disagreed with him politically to place their trust in Harold the man.

His great humanism has endeared him in all our hearts and for a long time his loss will be grievously felt. During the past months when overtaken by ill heath and deeply hurt by the death of Billie to whom he was devoted, he came to accept that his time was short, but concern for others remained as always his constant theme.

We who were privileged to work with him and enjoy his friendship salute his memory.

So we bid farewell to Harold Horne much loved friend, workmate and brother.

Farewell Harold Horne, soldier for democracy and indominatable fighter for Socialism.

International Brigade Association

from IBA chairman Bill Alexander
to Jill Jenkins, late daughter of Harold and Billie Horne

Dear Jill,

... Harold ... may have been in the fighting at QUINTO,
BELCHITE, MEDIANA, FUENTES DE EBRO, TERUEL, SEGURO
de LOS BANOS, THE BIG RETREAT, THE OFFENSIVE ACROSS
THE EBRO. He came home with the majority of the British
Battalion on 7 December 1938 and therefore would have been in the
final parade of the International Brigades in Barcelona. (All these
battles are described in the history I have written *'British Volunteers
for Liberty - Spain 1936-39'* published by Lawrence andWishart.
    I have to say 'may' because no records were kept saying when
comrades were wounded and in hospital, when they returned and so
on, and with a very high casualty rate – people were often wounded
two or three times away from the battalion until they recovered and
returned to the fighting. All that I can do is to ask any of our
comrades who were in action in the same period if they have any
memories of Harold. You will appreciate that after nearly fifty years
memories, of most of us, tend to lessen. I have only one memory –
small but very vivid. After the battle of Teruel where we were in
deep snow and freezing cold we were moved North towards Seguro
de los Banos. The weather changed, the sun was shining and we
took over front line positions from an Anarchist unit. I remember
going at night with Harold in a forward patrol while our trenches
were being deepened behind.
    The following afternoon, the sun was shining like a Spring day in
Britain and Harold came down the trench from the front line. We sat
in the sun discussing the front. I remember how young and fresh he
looked. He had some rank but I cannot remember, and there are no
existing records (they were lost or destroyed in the big retreat) ...
    Very best wishes
    Bill Alexander